Accidental Lessons

A Memoir of a Rookie Teacher and a Life Renewed

David W. Berner

 **Strategic Book Publishing**

Softcover edition published 2009.
Cloth cover and dust jacket edition published 2010

Strategic Book Publishing
An imprint of Strategic Book Group
P.O. Box 333
Durham, CT 06422
www.StrategicBookGroup.com

ISBN (cloth cover and dust jacket): 978-1-60976-411-1
ISBN (softcover): 978-1-60693-391-6

Book Design: Bruce Salender

Printed in the United States of America

For Casey and Graham

Acknowledgments

Many people urged me to write this book and were supportive throughout the long process. Thanks to Marie, Casey, and Graham. Thanks to my mother for continually asking me, "How's the writing going?" Thanks to Thomas E. Kennedy for his keen eye, expert talent, and encouraging words. And special thanks to the students at Cowherd Middle School who are the heart and soul of this book.

Note to the Reader

This book is one of memory, recollection, and what I believe to be my personal truth. I kept notes of my year as a rookie teacher, documenting moments, incidents, and exchanges at the public school where I worked. The stories told in this book are as I remember them. The recollections pertaining to my career as a journalist, my college years, and my days as a young boy have been confirmed through family members, acquaintances, and colleagues. The names of most adults and all of the students have been altered or changed to protect their privacy.

Stories based on memory can shift in the telling, change over time, and the best an author can hope for is that he illuminates the essence of what is true. To the best of my memory and ability, all that is reported here is correct and honest.

Since the authoring of this memoir, there has been significant academic progress reported at Cowherd Middle School in Aurora, Illinois. Those dedicated teachers and administrators who cared enough to create change for the children should be celebrated.

The price of anything is the amount of life you exchange for it.

Henry David Thoreau

Prologue

An undergraduate student of mine had no idea what to do.

"I know I'm supposed to have the idea this week," he said, missing the deadline for a class assignment. "But, I just don't have any good ones. I don't have any stories to tell."

This was a senior-level Radio Documentary class at the college where I teach, requiring students to produce a short, personal story about a subject that illuminates the human condition—the essence of documentary. But sometimes discovering that story, developing it into a rich narrative that enlightens or provokes is a tough task.

"You do have a story to tell. We just have to find it," I said.

I asked him to go home and think hard about what he believed was important to him, what made his heart pound, his eyes water, his soul lift.

He shook his head and rolled his eyes. "I don't know," he said. "I never think about that stuff."

When I was a young boy I wanted to be Jacques Cousteau, the oceanographer whose 1960s TV specials carried the viewer on fantastic voyages below the surface of the deep, vast sea. I watched those programs with a dreamer's intensity, simultaneously drawing pictures of underwater divers and never-seen-before one-eyed ocean creatures that I, as a famous explorer, would some day encounter and photograph with a one-of-a-kind, specially designed underwater camera.

Years later, I wanted to be Stephen Stills from the 70s group Crosby, Stills and Nash. I dreamed of playing guitar in his bluesy, acoustic style and singing songs with a voice as smoky as his. Then, it was Jimmy Roach, the disc jockey on the album-rock station in Pittsburgh where I grew up. Roach had the voice of God, deep like the seas Cousteau explored. I wanted to be like Jimmy, on the radio, playing the music I loved, telling the stories of the artists whose lyrics mattered so much to an impressionistic teenager.

My student hadn't figured out yet what mattered to him. Wasn't even close. Decide what he wanted to do with his life? What he wanted to be? He was still trying to figure out how to fulfill the requirements for the class assignment. He had far to go.

And so did I.

Although, in my teenage years, I thought I knew how my life should unfold, what I wanted to be, the reality was that I hadn't thought about it hard enough, hadn't lived, experienced enough. As I've told the students in my documentary class, you have to learn to "go deep." It's a phrase I often used to stress how important it is to strip away the layers and get to the soul of the story, the essence of it. It has to resonate somewhere deeper, deeper than you've been before. It's not an easy endeavor. Digging far below the surface can get you into unfamiliar, even scary territory, corners of your psyche that are sometimes dark and murky, like some of the places in Cousteau's oceans.

But of course, as a young man, I didn't know this. It took living, the daily movement through the days, for me to finally begin to understand that you can't live your life on the surface; you have to strap on the air tank and dive in if you want to discover what you're all about, what matters.

The next week, my student reported to class early, bursting

to tell me what he had discovered.

"I did a lot of thinking and I believe I got it."

"Did you 'go deep?'" I said.

"Yep, and I know the story I want to tell."

We sat down alone, next to each other in the hard-plastic classroom chairs.

"I run the Chicago Marathon each year," he said. "And I want to do something about the training, the work that goes into it."

"Well," I said, trying to be encouraging but honest, "that's more of a feature story, not really a personal documentary."

"I knew you would say that," he said, smiling. "That's when I remembered to 'go deep.'"

"*Why* you run the marathon?"

"Exactly. And here is why," he said more seriously, pausing to carefully consider his words. "I run the marathon because of my father."

I leaned into him from my chair. "Tell me more," I said.

"My father is not well. He has heart problems. He needs to take better care of himself. And the real reason I run the marathon is to show Dad that anyone can rebuild their health, turn their life around."

He sat back in his chair, lingering in the moment.

"It's not that I want to show off or accomplish some athletic, personal goal. I run the marathon because I want to show my father the possibilities," he said. "My father is my best friend."

He had found his story.

I didn't tell him that discovering a narrative, *going deep* and exposing the things that matter, is rarely simple or painless. You don't figure it all out over a weekend. I didn't tell him that one day you want to be Jacques Cousteau and the next Stephen Stills, and never come close to either. I didn't tell him that the stories of your life change and shift, are altered by unforeseen encounters, moments, and molded by comedies and tragedies, and that the lessons can come completely by accident. I didn't tell him that I once had been where he is.

Just a day before this student was to graduate, the radio department held a reception for our seniors. It was a simple get-together with cans of Coke and paper plates of crackers and cheese. Parents were invited, and that's where I met my student's father, the focus of his documentary story.

"Dad, this is Mr. Berner," he said. "He helped me tell the story about you and the marathon."

"Honored to meet you," I said. "Your son thinks a lot of you."

"It was a pretty good story, wasn't it?" he said, a bit embarrassed by the attention.

My student smiled nervously and took a sip of his soda.

"It was quite brave of your son to open up his heart and show so much vulnerability," I said to the father. "Telling stories like that takes some courage."

"Yeah, he's a good kid."

Later that evening, as the reception was ending and everyone was leaving for the night, my student came to me to say good-bye, to shake my hand, and ask if he could trouble me with a question.

He leaned into me and whispered, "How did you know what you wanted to do with your life?"

Graduating students had asked me that many times. But on this night, it felt like a brand-new question.

"I am certainly not the guru for something that profound," I said. "But you might want to think about what got you to the heart of your story about the marathon and your father."

"Go deep?" he asked, already knowing the answer.

"Yes, go deep."

"Have you *gone deep*, Mr. Berner?" he said, smiling at the intimacy of the question and the potential answer.

I suddenly saw him as a friend, not as a student, and felt in that single moment as if we were at the center of an intersection of the past and the future. I saw him in me, and me in him. I saw my father. I saw my sons.

I never responded to his question, only to answer it silently in my head.

"Have you *gone deep*, Mr. Berner?"
Oh, deeper than you can ever imagine.

Chapter 1

The very first student on my very first day of teaching barreled into the middle school classroom, spinning, eyes darting.

"What's up, fuckers?"

The boy, black-haired, with a wiry build, and short for his age, clearly enjoyed the shock value, but obviously had expected to unload his question into a roomful of students. Instead, he got only me. Without eye contact, but completely aware of my presence, he bolted out of the room before I could reprimand him, question him, even say a word, then quickly weaved his way through the packed hallway. His body ricocheted off lockers, walls, and students as if he were a rubber bumper car in an amusement park ride. I stood just outside my classroom door and watched as he spun and bounded back toward my end of the hall.

"Diego!" shouted one student and then another, and another, all clearly annoyed by his antics. Diego laughed, almost maniacally, and then grabbed a handful of the nearest girl's backside.

"Di-e-go!" she said as she swung her arm, hoping to hit him.

Diego was too fast. He was already down the hall past a

second row of lockers. He suddenly stopped and stood next to another student, staring at him. It was excruciating for Diego to be still; he quivered with energy.

"You're gay, aren't you?" Diego reveled in startling people.

"Get the hell out of here, you dickhead." The student said this almost routinely, as if he'd heard it all before.

Diego was gone. Didn't stay to hear the response. He knew what it would be. He dashed through the glass doors at the near end of the hall and was back outside. I could see him, standing on the sidewalk, his head snapping back and forth as he quickly surveyed what was in his sight, like a nervous bird. Then, he zigged and zagged his way out of view and vanished into the crowd of students.

"Diego obviously hasn't had his meds," said Mrs. Murray, the eighth grade's lead teacher, matter-of-factly. She supervised the team of teachers in my wing of the school and had been around for years, maybe decades. She saw it all, heard it all, and knew Diego and the details of his distressed and dysfunctional life all too well. "You got him first period, right?"

"Ah, yeah," I said as I continued to process what I had witnessed. My eyes were still locked on the glass doors as I considered how in the hell I was going to deal with that kid.

"Make sure you talk to the nurse," said Mrs. Murray. "She has to give him his pills. But his crazy family may not have done anything yet about getting the drugs to the school."

More students crammed into the halls. I took my eyes away from the door while Mrs. Murray filled in Diego's story.

"Weird situation he's in. Dad and Mom are divorced, but the dad still lives in the same house, with his girlfriend. Diego lives in the middle of it all. Everybody's always fighting. They don't have any money."

"Wow," I said, softly.

Welcome to day one at Cowherd Middle School.

Just a few months before this August morning, I was living in my pajamas. Good, comfortable, mixed-matched, makeshift sleepwear made of flannel and cotton. The pants oversized, faded gray plaid with a drawstring to hold them up, and the shirt was a simple black T-shirt from Target—one that had seen far too many wash cycles. It was the perfect daily wardrobe for an out-of-work journalist who, among other delights of aimlessness, had discovered TV's *The Price is Right* could be a pretty solid companion. "Come on down!" became so familiar to me, I developed a new, although not very enviable, skill—shouting the show's signature phrase at precisely the same time as the announcer. Got it right on the money every time. Bob Barker, MTV, VH-1, The Golf Channel, ESPN, and at least one daily soap opera, I can't remember the name, became my best buddies. We'd meet over coffee, with sugar and light cream, and sometimes later in the afternoon, a little Jameson Irish whiskey in a clear juice glass. I never got drunk. Sometimes, though, I wish I had.

Diego wasn't the only one making memorable first impressions. There was the girl with ten piercings in one ear, the thirteen-year-old boy who easily weighed close to three hundred pounds and towered over me in his giant frame, and the overwhelming sense of poverty. As a hedge against gang influences, gang colors, the students wore mandatory uniforms—white or blue T-shirt, and blue or white pants—but many of the white shirts were worn thin, grayed or yellowed, and permanently stained from years of wear. The blue in the blue jeans mixed with the brown and black of grease and dirt. But, despite the ragged clothing, there were smiles and laughter, and plenty of both in the hallways that morning. Many of the students had known each other since elementary school and lived in the same neighborhoods. Girls hugged each other hello, boys slapped one another on the back or playfully wrestled, roughhoused. They knew the teachers, too, greeting Mrs. Murray and the others as they walked by the classroom doors where each of us stood guard. For me, though, well, I felt a bit like the new neighbor invited to the annual block party, a bit of an outsider.

"You a teacher?" said a boy with a shaved head and an earring.

"Yep. Mr. Berner," I said, sticking out my hand for a shake. "You are?"

The student was obviously unaccustomed to such a gesture. He had no idea what to do with my hand. After a moment of confusion, he placed his palm meekly into mine, offered a fish-like handshake, and quickly pulled away.

"Arturo," he said, looking left and right as if he had a secret he wanted to share with only me. "Hey, what kind of music you like? I can download anything for you. Burn it. Get you a CD. I won't charge you much. Let me know."

Arturo had a business going. He illegally downloaded songs from the Internet, put them on CDs, and sold them to students and others. On this morning he was trying to expand his client base. He didn't see me as a teacher; he saw me as a customer. Arturo, like many others, came from a humble family, and that made me wonder about the computer and the gear he needed to do this little under-the-table job of his, especially in the days before iTunes and iPods. How was he doing it? I probably didn't want to know.

My last real work was with an online golf publication, as a senior writer and reporter. It was a great gig, while it lasted. I wrote for the South African-based Internet company for about five months, making decent money, but the dicey business plan crumbled when the bottom fell out of the dot-com boom in the mid-1990s, and all the company's funding disintegrated. After more than two months without a paycheck, I received the legal notice in the mail that the company was going bankrupt.

Before the Internet job, it was years of covering the news as a broadcast reporter, mostly radio. It was work that had become sickeningly routine and increasingly influenced by corporate accountants who had taken over much of the broadcast industry. Writers were laid off, reporters were forced to become desk assistants and taken off their beats, the money we once had for advertising radio stations was yanked away, and when field sound recording equipment broke down, it was repaired, in patchwork fashion, over and over and over like a teenager's junk car. As news gatherers, we were asked to produce more stories with less time for inquiry and fact-checking. It was sloppy and hurried reporting, and few managers seemed to care. These were battles I kept fighting, and it wore me out, dulled my senses. I learned to hate the job.

"Hey, mister," another student called from across the hall as he shut his locker door. "Whatta you teach? And what's with the tie?" I had thought wearing a tie might show some authority. In the early going, it wasn't working. In time, the tie became part of my teaching persona.

His name was Sergio. A pimply-faced boy with what appeared to be a perpetual grin, a goofy smile born out of a mixture of devilment and immaturity. There was a shyness about him, even though he asked bold questions of a man he had never met before.

"This first period I'm teaching social studies, but mostly language arts. You in this class?" I said.

"I don't know. Lost my schedule," he said, still sporting that goofy smile.

"You going to the office?"

"I guess. What's your name?"

"Mr. Berner."

"You hard?"

"Depends."

"I stink at school."

"I'll bet you do okay."

"No. I stink. My mother says I better pass."

"We'll give it a shot, Sergio. You better head for the office and get a copy of your schedule."

He turned in the direction of friends who had called out his name, and left without saying anything else to me. I later discovered Sergio was reading at the second grade level, could barely write a simple sentence, and would constantly lose homework, notebooks, textbooks, and never, ever came to class with a pencil. But that grin was like a tattoo, permanent.

There were no bells that signaled the start of the school day at Cowherd. Instead, teachers would look at the industrial wall clocks and yell down the hallways, "Let's go. Time for class. Break it up, guys. Let's go." We were sheepdogs herding students into the classrooms and to their desks. I watched the other teachers doing it, so I did it, too.

Just outside my door a crowd of five girls talked with great animation; facial expressions changed by the second, and arms and hands accented each vocal burst. They ignored the orders to get to class. Instead, they groomed. One combed another's hair. Drugstore perfume overtook the oxygen.

"Okay, ladies. Let's go."

Two left, three kept talking.

"Ladies," I said with a firmer tone.

One more left and two remained.

"Come on, girls," I croaked one last time.

That's when I got the Lucia stare.

Lucia liked to play the part of the tough girl. She walked with purpose in the hallways and sneered at other students, teachers, anyone. She enjoyed the role and certainly wasn't going to change for some lame, new teacher. Lucia tried to stare me down, glared, and slowly turned. She refused to take her eyes away from mine. They were locked on me like those of a stalking animal claiming its territory, proving its dominance.

Her friend Elena had already defiantly stamped her feet, rolled her eyes, sighed with disgust, and twisted around, leaving the two of us alone. Elena, I would later learn, absolutely hated any authority over her, but she dealt with it differently than her friend. Lucia confronted authority, showing open defiance and distrust. Elena, on the other hand, avoided confrontation but made sure you knew she wasn't happy with having to listen to anyone telling her what to do.

Lucia's silence was palpable. Her eyes bored into mine as she inched backward toward the far lockers. I stayed with her, my eyes glued to hers. I knew if I backed down it would signal a victory for her, and I couldn't let that happen. She disappeared into the classroom two doors down. At that moment, if you would have told me Lucia and I would someday reach an understanding, a common respect, I never would have believed it.

A few other students were still in the hallway, scurrying to get to class before teachers shut the doors. One student snuck in under my arm as I pulled my classroom door closed, and then in rushed Diego.

"Hey!" he blurted as he squeezed through the now narrow opening. He spun, stood momentarily still, and glared directly at me.

"You smoke weed?"

I paused for what seemed like an eternal moment. It was one of the many random, seemingly disconnected questions Diego would lay on me over the school year.

"Come on, let's go, have a seat," I said as I ushered him in.

"You always been bald?"

"Hey, Diego." Mr. Cruz, the instructor who was assigned to team-teach the first period social studies class with me, had had enough. "Cut it out. Have a seat. Come here." Mr. Cruz knew Diego enough to direct him calmly, without emotion.

"Just asking a question," Diego said, as if someone were violating First Amendment rights. He plopped himself in the nearest seat and began nervously drumming the desk with his knuckles. Without missing a beat, out came another question.

"You like porn?"

I made a note to talk to the nurse.

There was no doubt about it. I was now planted inside what was reported to be one of the Chicago area's most troubled school districts—East Aurora, District 131—with difficult, sometimes unruly students; poor students from broken, dysfunctional families, some with histories of violence, crime, and neglect. I knew, rather vaguely, what I was getting into when I agreed to take the job, but on this first day it was quite apparent I didn't have a clue what I was doing. Still, through it all, I maintained a sliver of self-belief that I could do something good here. It was unnerving, even scary, but at the same time invigorating, and the only way to find

looked at me, as if searching for some sense of security.

"Dad? What's happening here?"

Casey knew this wasn't going to be the usual after-dinner talk.

"It's okay," I said, reaching again for Casey's hand. This time he squeezed back.

Graham looked up from his plate. "Who died?" he said. It was a running joke in the family to ask that question whenever conversations got too serious, and Graham was usually the first to joke.

"You've probably noticed Mom and Dad haven't been staying, sleeping, in the same room in the house," Marie said. "And maybe you've seen some, well, tension between us."

"Yeah, pretty obvious, Mom. You guys aren't getting a divorce, are you?" Graham asked this as if to dismiss the answer. But as much as Marie and I tried to keep our lives appearing normal in the household, it was now obvious the boys hadn't missed much.

I moved my hand from Casey's and onto his shoulder, now stiff and tense. His face turned away from the table. He knew what the answer to Graham's question would be.

"Mom and Dad still love each other," Marie said as she reached for Graham. "I will always love your father."

"And I...I will always love your mother," I said.

Graham now knew the reality of the moment. Quick as he was to humor, he was also quick to show emotion, and tears formed in his eyes. Marie stood to wrap her arms around him. Casey refused to look at any of us.

"We're still going to get together for holidays, I will find a place close by to live, and you can both stay there anytime." I tried to be comforting, reaching for Casey, trying to get him to look at me. I stroked Graham's hair and ran my hand on his cheek. "I'll get a dog. It'll be okay."

Casey pounded his fist on the table; his eyes filled with water. Graham kept crying, his body shaking. Marie held him tighter.

Marie and I continued to talk, trying to give the boys some

belief, some hope, that we could make this work for everyone, that we wouldn't be the typical divorced family. Mom and Dad weren't angry with each other, certainly didn't hate each other, and were absolutely committed to keeping their lives the center of ours. But, for now, very little of this mattered. The word "divorce" simply couldn't be masked. The word, the coming changes, drained the innocence away.

I stayed up late that night; I couldn't sleep. Sat on the outside porch in the chill and dark, too exhausted to rest my head. What kind of father was I? Who does this to their kids? My parents had troubles, but they stuck it out. Was I weak? Was Marie being unreasonable? And why now, when I was about to begin graduate work, a new career, a new part of my life? What kind of father considers how he's going to relate to unknown kids from a poor Hispanic neighborhood, when his own children are crying out for comfort, stability, and the remaining piece of the secure and happy home they thought they had?

I had messed up my life, and my boys were hurting for it.

Chapter 3

I grew up wanting to be a rock star, even playing in a garage band during high school and college days. We actually practiced in my parents' basement, not the garage, so you might say that put us a step above the typical teenage band. Plus, years of piano lessons and teaching myself the guitar gave me and my three school buddies enough confidence and reasonable skills to bang out some Eagles, The Rolling Stones, and even, reluctantly, the wedding reception favorite—Alley Cat. But playing dive clubs, teen dances, and shotgun weddings wasn't exactly rock star status. The next best thing might be to broadcast the music I loved on the radio—minus Alley Cat.

I was a less than average singer, but I had a decent speaking voice.

"You should be on the radio," people would say. "Your voice is so strong, deep."

It was my father's voice. I sounded just like him.

During my undergraduate days, I made my way onto the college radio station, where I spun the hits and album cuts of the day, literally, on the vinyl 45s and 33s—Led Zeppelin, Bob Dylan, Steve Miller, CSNY, Dan Fogelberg, and Steely Dan.

Radio quickly became all I thought about, cared about. It was the perfect mix of playing and talking about the music I loved.

"Dylan certainly influenced a generation of songwriters. But he also was the subject of song lyrics. Dylan is believed to be the 'Jester' in Don McLean's song 'American Pie.'" This is how I filled the spaces between the songs. I knew artists' backgrounds, trivia about their early days as singers and songwriters, and stories about how and why songs were written.

"'Hey Jude,' legend has it, was written for John Lennon's son, Julian. But Paul McCartney felt the title 'Hey Jules' just wasn't going to work."

I searched for radio stations that would hire a rock-crazed kid with shoulder-length hair, and nothing but Levi's and flannel and T-shirts in his wardrobe, and a passion, a belief that music, my music, could change the world. That radio station was in McKeesport, Pennsylvania, a tired, old steel town about forty miles from where I grew up, Pittsburgh.

I was hired over the phone.

"Your demo tape sounds good," the program director told me. He liked my "pipes"—the slang term used in the business for one's voice—and liked my relatively easy on-air manner. He thought I sounded real, not so much like a traditional announcer. Remember Gary Owens? The actor who created the parody of an announcer on the old TV show *Laugh-In*? I was *not* Gary Owens. "You want to work early Saturday mornings? Play songs, read liners, give the weather, basic stuff?"

During the late 1960s, WIXZ had been a successful Top-40 radio station, but it was now surviving with another format—the music of Merle Haggard, Conway Twitty, and Crystal Gayle—country. Not exactly this rock-n-roller's dream, but it was an on-air job in radio, my first one, plus I would make four dollars an hour. I was rich.

"Is it really four dollars an hour?" I asked, stunned I could be paid that much money.

"Look," he said, sternly, "I can get someone else." He thought I was trying to negotiate, like some arrogant, big-time radio star.

"Oh, no, four bucks is great." I was certain I could get comfortable with country music.

For two years, I lived with, and even learned to enjoy, the twang of this quintessentially American music. After all, a lot of rock-n-roll came from the blues, just like much of early country-western music. I talked about it, promoted it, and studied it, and got good enough to be hired at another country station in the area, and it was there I was asked to make a big career shift—develop a news department for the station. Me? News? I had no journalism in my blood, but management saw something in me that gave them confidence I could make this happen. More likely, they just needed a warm body to handle the work, for four dollars an hour.

After a few years of stumbling through radio stations trying to find my journalistic way, I eventually developed into a pretty good newsman working for radio stations in Pittsburgh and Chicago, freelancing for major networks—CBS, ABC, CNN, and National Public Radio—covering politics, tornado disasters, murders, and scandals, and winning awards and accolades. I even cut my hair—to the earlobes.

It was solid, challenging, rewarding work, for a time. My curiosity about the music I loved turned to curiosity about the world around me. But after nearly twenty years of chasing stories, the industry had changed. Broadcasting was now run by accountants, not the creative programmers and news people I had learned from. It had become a product of the revenue, investment-driven, greedy 1980s, and I was a product of a different decade. I wanted something new, meaningful. I ached for new challenges, something beyond fires, murders, and daily politics. And certainly something deeper than what management found most important—the bottom line.

But I was stymied by my own inability to take a step forward and search out something fresh, rewarding. I was stuck between the comfortable life I had created, and one that would sound a deeper chord. Marie, for years, witnessed my stagnation, my struggle, and there came a time when nearly every day, she would encourage me to find a new path, sometimes insist on it. One night, she demanded I do something.

"David, you are just not happy," Marie said after enduring an evening walk, one on which I hadn't said a word for nearly forty-five minutes. I was a voiceless mope.

"I'm fine, Marie, really," I said, trying to avoid the subject. I didn't bother to look at her.

She stopped walking, stepped in front of me, put her hands on my shoulders, as if she was about to shake me, and looked straight into my eyes, forcing me to look back. "You've come to hate what you do, you're miserable, it's making me miserable, and you have to change. Find another job, find something." She was pleading with me, trying to get inside my head and stir up buried enthusiasm.

"What the hell am I supposed to do?" I was annoyed and frustrated. "This is all I know. I've been doing it for two decades, never wanted to do anything else but be on the radio. I don't know how to do anything else." I tried to get her to keep walking, give up the conversation. She wouldn't have it.

"I don't think you get it," Marie said, putting her hands on my cheeks and moving her face closer to mine as if the intimacy would make things more urgent.

"I get it. But what am I going to do? Get a job for twenty grand? We can't do that."

"David. I don't care what you do, but you have to make a move, any move. It's ripping you apart and it's wearing on me, really wearing on me."

We lived in a comfortable four-bedroom colonial in the suburbs. It was "Leave It to Beaver" stuff. I cut the lawn on Sundays, went to barbeques with the neighbors, and lived what many would call an idyllic American life. But, as with most men, my identity came from my career and my status. It was sexy to do what I did for a living, I got attention, and people loved to ask me questions about the stories I covered, the work I did.

"Have you ever interviewed someone really important?" one new neighbor asked me as we were introducing ourselves the day his family moved in.

"Depends on who you think is important, I guess." I always felt a bit uncomfortable answering those questions. I didn't want to appear a self-important braggart.

"I did interview Bill Gates once. Ted Kennedy, Jimmy Carter," I answered.

"You're kidding," he said, amazed that I had actually talked to the people he read about in the newspapers. "What's Gates like?"

They always asked about Gates.

"He really is a geek. Loves playing video, computer games."

I regularly received complimentary tickets to baseball games and the theater, invitations to interesting parties and gala openings. To many, I had a dream job. But to me, it was smoke and mirrors, an illusion of something more real.

The radio station that first hired me in Chicago, WMAQ, was struggling. The number of listeners had slipped and revenue was down, and for months there had been speculation it would close its doors, unheard of in the business. I was going to be out of a job. The loss of the full-time radio work propelled me into writing for the golf website. When that fizzled, along came the Mr. Mom days. Thinking back, I am convinced the time off from meaningful work did me damage. I lost myself and eventually lost my wife. But just as the marriage was ending, something new was beginning.

I applied to a graduate school program at Aurora University, hoping it might revitalize me. It was too late to save my marriage, but maybe a new challenge could save me.

The program at the college, ten miles from my home and forty miles west of Chicago, was designed to accelerate the qualification process for the Illinois certification to teach in the public schools. Still, I wasn't completely sold on the idea. The pay was abysmal, and I was reluctant to go back to school, commit myself to it, and justify the time it would take to prepare myself academically. I used excuses like that for years. I was pretty good at excuses.

The program was designed to recruit the professional, the person with "real life" experience who wanted to bring his skills to the classroom. It was a sanitized public relations attempt at delivering education. Administrators at the school would never admit the obvious: finding experienced teachers, good teachers, for lousy schools was nearly impossible. Plus, I couldn't just walk in and get started. I had to be accepted. But if I passed the application process, the district would place me in a classroom, pay me, and at the same time, send me through the graduate classes with scholarship money to help. This was a no-brainer, at least in theory, especially since I was without a steady job, and about to be divorced and alone for the first time in twelve years.

Still, teaching was far off course from my early dreams. And actually being accepted into the program and then into a classroom required some hurdle jumps.

It was a weekday, and as on most other weekdays due to my off and on work pattern, I was in my familiar stay-at-home-dad routine—making my kids' lunches for the next school day—one sandwich with peanut butter only, one with jelly and peanut butter, two Oreo cookies in each, one with a red Braeburn apple, one with a Granny Smith.

"Mr. Berner, we're sorry to inform you that you were not chosen as one of the Transition to Teaching cohort members." The female voice on the phone, a clerk or assistant dean, was emotionless, robotic.

"Oh, I see," I said, surprised and disappointed. "I'm sorry to hear that." It took a second to settle in. "Can you tell me why?"

"You'll have to take that up with someone in the School of Education. Give them a phone call. They'll have more information."

It was done. I was not one of the few people picked from some four hundred applicants. For a moment, I considered making the phone call that would explain it all, but quickly gave up the idea. "The hell with it," I said to myself. Nothing else was going very well in my life; why should this?

Two days later, there was another telephone call.

"Mr. Berner, we just wanted to let you know the first meeting of the Transition to Teaching cohort will be next week."

What?

Apparently the clerk who had been asked to do the dirty work had screwed up. Instead of telephoning those who *weren't* chosen, she had called all of those who *were* and informed them they had been rejected. Whoops. I would soon learn that administrative bloopers in the public schools happened on a regular basis.

The initial call had only justified my increasingly sour existence, all rather appropriate for my current state of mind. But the second, well, that may have been the single most important call of my life. Maybe there was a challenge here that would renew me.

Too bad it wasn't that simple. What happened next nearly made me give up before I could start.

It was a Saturday morning in February, chilly not frigid, unusual for Chicago, and I was on my way to the inaugural meeting of cohort members. I dressed up a bit, Friday casual, and carried a note pad and a pen. Maybe a little nerdy when I think of it now, but I was pumped up, feeling pretty good about myself that morning, for a change, reasonably optimistic about what could be ahead.

Just a few blocks from the university, my cell phone rang. It was the CBS-owned station where I was freelancing.

"Dave, where are you?"

The voice was direct, firm, urgent.

"The shuttle, Columbia, disintegrated coming in for a landing, all likely dead. We need bodies in the newsroom."

Every instinct I had, every nerve, trained for decades, encouraged me to turn around, head for the station, and move into battle mode. That's what broadcast journalists do. We move *toward* the big story, not away from it. I eased on the brakes, immediately pulled the car to the curb, and thought, *Turn around, head toward the newsroom. It's what you do.*

"Dave, you need to be here as soon as possible." The editor was now directing me, insisting I take action.

I said nothing.

"Dave?" he said.

I stayed quiet.

"Hello? Dave?"

"I can't help." The words shot from my mouth as if some-one had finally pulled the trigger. "I'm scheduled at a meeting at Aurora University and I can't miss it. Seriously, I have to go. Sorry."

I offered suggestions on other staffers to call and pushed the phone's end-call button. I sat motionless in my car, shaken by what I had done. In my entire career, I had never before said no to a story.

The meeting at the university was far from what I expected. There was a hitch, one that could make or break things. Not all the cohort members were going to get classrooms to work in; not all would have jobs or get paid. Some of us would have to student-teach, and that meant no paychecks.

I felt like I'd been punched. This new wrinkle was not ne-gotiable. I was closing in on a final divorce, and planning to move to my own place. I needed the work. All these things would be impossible with a no-pay student teaching assign-ment. I was angry.

I stayed through all the speakers, sitting in the back of the room with my arms crossed. My heart sank. What in the world was I going to do now? Why hadn't I just covered the shuttle story? It was too late now. Any twinge of excitement I had mustered for this new challenge had quickly evaporated. Still, something gnawed at me. Deep in the crevices of my head, my heart, there was, surprisingly, a dim and meager candle of op-timism. I thought, *Am I absolutely sure this isn't going to work out? I should speak to someone directly, a dean, an administra-tor, somebody, about what the chances really are of getting one of those now scarce teaching jobs. I was there, might as well ask, at least, at worst, it would confirm my own demise.*

"Excuse me." I approached the dean of the School of Edu-cation as the potential teachers and speakers began to file out the doors. I introduced myself and got to the point. "I need to know for sure whether I've been assigned to a school or not."

"Oh, Mr. Berner, you're set for Cowherd Middle School. We have you scheduled to begin teaching in the fall, eighth grade, language arts at Cowherd. It's on the northeast side of town."

The university chose more than a dozen cohort members, but only half were guaranteed a teaching job. I was one of them.

Three of the biggest changes of my life were now beginning to take palpable shape—teaching, divorce, and the news my father was receiving inside a doctor's office five hundred miles away.

Chapter 4

During that summer, my boys had been playing Little League baseball and I was the manager, the head coach. It was a rather sorry lot; *Bad News Bears*, you might say. We had just three or four kids who could routinely catch a grounder, not get lost in the dandelion outfields, and knew they could run past first base without being tagged out. No All-Stars, by any means. One kid would routinely sit down in the outfield during the middle of a game.

"Dad," Casey said to me from the dugout one early season game. "Riley is now lying down out there!"

"Riley!" he yelled.

"Let me handle it, Case," I said. But Casey was clearly disgusted.

"Riley, you want to get up, son?" I said.

He looked up from a sitting position, waved, and slowly stood, only to face the wrong direction. Not toward the field, but toward the right-field fence.

My two boys were at least reasonable players. They could hold their own. Of course, remember, I was their father. But, in the bigger picture, it didn't really matter how good, committed, or motivated these kids were about baseball, including my own. I just wanted them to learn a little and go home after the last inning with a smile on their faces.

My dad was a coach, too, when I was a little guy playing on those ragged toddler teams back in Pennsylvania. The Little League teams of my era were less about inclusion and teaching the fundamentals and more about raw talent. If you couldn't catch a fly ball, tag out a runner, hit a solid shot to left, throw a reasonable curve, you weren't going to play much. And there was no coddling. If you didn't get the job done, you learned to like the bench. If you were hurt, well, you just rubbed some dirt on it and got back in the game.

"Dave, I know it hurts, but you have to tough it out," my dad said after a wicked bad-hop grounder ripped a gash in my lower lip. Blood was on my uniform; an ice bag was planted firmly on my mouth.

"But, Dad, what if it happens again?" I mumbled through my quivering lips, now swollen and salty from the tears that had mixed with dirt on my cheeks and settled in the corners of my mouth.

I was just eight years old, and a stinger to short caught me not looking.

"I want you to get back out there, Dave," Dad said. "If you don't, you'll always be afraid of the ball. That can't happen, right?"

"But, Dad."

"You can do this, Dave. Sit out an inning, then back to shortstop. You'll be fine."

He pulled the ice bag away to get a look at my lip, now purple from the gathering bruise and puffed out like a blowfish.

"The bleeding's stopped. How's it feel?" Dad asked.

"Stings, feels weird," I mumbled.

"Keep the ice on it. Here's your glove. Sit on the bench. We'll get you out there next inning."

I didn't want to go back, but I knew Dad was right. He didn't want me to crumble under my fears, my worries. He wanted me to face them. I know all this now. Then? Well, I was eight.

Nearly forty years later, I was facing a very different fear, the fear of a major life change. The end of my marriage was near, all done but the paperwork, the final signatures before the judge. One good thing, the usual financial negotiations were nearly painless, not to mention unusual. Marie and I had worked out the details on our own, no warring attorneys battling for pieces of our lives. She got the house and gave me a large chunk of her savings; the boys would live with her as not to shake up their lives any more than necessary; and visitation was worked out solely between us. There was no official court order. The only time an attorney was hired was when we needed one to represent us before the judge in divorce court. "Highly unconventional" is what the judge called our divorce agreement, but he agreed, after a myriad of questions, to sign off on it. It was all so civilized.

"You don't have to leave, David. Not yet," Marie told me over a glass of wine late one weekend night after a long evening of sad, but forgiving talk. "Stay, find your footing, get your graduate work going, and teaching. I want you to be okay."

We weren't ever going to be the typical divorced couple. Mutual respect was still there, still deep in us both. And we had the boys. They would link us forever, no matter the scars.

"Let's ease into the changes. It'll be better for you, me, and the kids," she said.

There were a lot of things to think about, and I was in no rush to leave. Also, the inevitable was on my mind: Where would I go? What could I afford? Where would I live?

For weeks Marie never mentioned my eventual move, never asked if I had a time frame, not once. I appreciated that. I had much to consider. I prepared for my days in graduate school, buying notebooks and textbooks, getting my student ID. I attended university meetings, and continued my freelance work, along with a househusband's list of chores. I was busy with something new, maybe even exciting. It felt good, and the nearly debilitating tension of the uncertainties of our marriage had vanished. I didn't like what was before us, but at least I knew what I was up against.

"I want to show you something." Marie was in the driver's seat of her car; I was in the passenger seat. She turned the corner off the main four-lane street and into the heart of our neighborhood. We had been out to a weekend lunch together, catching up a bit on each other's lives. We still lived in the same house, but a couple of months had passed now, and her job, my new focus, the kids, school, and certainly our marital status—separated, but not really—kept us from physically splitting.

She drove her Saab down the street two blocks from our home, past the single-family houses and onto a section of the block where duplexes took over. They were comfortable places, three- bedroom, neatly kept, nothing fancy. I had driven or walked by them a hundred times before. She pulled the car over and drifted it to a stop in front of a white-sided home with a red door and an attached two-car garage. On the front lawn was a for-sale sign.

"What do you think?" she said, her voice tentative, cracking a bit.

It was an unexpected detour and unanticipated question. Confusion caused hesitation.

"These are pretty nice," she said, subtly attempting to persuade while nodding her head at the house. "The kids would be very close. They could walk to your house, and you would be close for me. I know I'll have a lot of travel for work, and being just down the street would be good for everyone."

I was not in the habit of having my wife, soon-to-be ex-wife, taking me out to look at homes for sale. This was a new experience, yet familiar. Marie was an organizer, a caregiver. It was her nature to make certain everyone was all right.

"I can't believe you're now my real estate agent," I said, softly, slowly beginning to cry, and trying to lighten the moment with a half laugh.

"I want you to feel good about where you live," she said, her eyes glistening, aching for me to agree, to at least consider this scenario.

We stayed in the car for nearly a half hour, mixing the raw emotion of our failed marriage with reality, practicality; we talked about how to move forward with our lives separately, and together. And there before us was a simple white house that someday could be my new home.

Rather unusual, don't you think? The ex-wife so involved in the future of her ex-husband, even directly guiding him to the purchase of a home. But, as you might have figured out, I was having problems moving forward with my life in so many ways and was happy to take all the help I could get.

That day, I felt closer to Marie than I had felt in a long time.

Over and over again, I wondered how I was able to get through these tough times. I'm surprised I didn't crumble from the weight of it all. And I wonder if Dad didn't have a part in it. Over time, as I grew up, my father may have subtly, incrementally shaped me for hard times like these. It wasn't a calculated plan; it was intuitive, and driven, at least partially, by Dad's past. His father left his mother when he was in high school, moved out to live with another woman, a woman who lived in the neighborhood, the mother of one of his friends. It was humiliating. Dad's father disappeared from his life when he was just a boy, and my dad's son was going to have a father, one who would love him, be proud of him, and show him how to grow up. Something he never had.

Dad's attempts to toughen me up came in spurts, and were never overwhelming. But when he did it, it made a definitive impression—like overcoming the baseball to the lip—and the time he told me to whack the biggest kid at the school bus stop over the head with my lunchbox.

The kid was enormous. It was fifth grade, and he was easily two hundred pounds.

"Hey, you're stupid. Stupid. Really stupid. But you know that, don't you? Sure you do, you stupid, stupid kid."

He said this, or something like it, nearly every morning as I walked to the bus stop. This monster kid would stay a couple of steps behind me and verbally jab me all the way up the hill from my house, past the modest brick homes and the tiny front lawns to the street corner. I tried to ignore it, but after a couple of weeks, I needed advice. I turned to Dad.

"Oh, for God's sake," he said, taking his eyes momentarily away from his newspaper. "Bash the kid over the head with your lunchbox." Dad didn't really mean for me to hit him, just to somehow shake it off, tough it out—the bully will get tired of it at some point. But when you're a kid, the world is very literal.

I hit the kid so hard I broke my thermos.

Talk about surprising yourself. I couldn't believe I had the guts to do it. And then, I was surprised again to watch the tormentor go mute. He stared at me, stunned, and rubbed his head. I doubt I hurt him, but I certainly got his attention. And what now? Should I run? Hit him again?

I heard the school bus rumbling toward our stop. And although I was still afraid of what the big guy might do, I simply walked away to the corner. The bully said nothing as he followed behind me. We never said another word to each other— at the bus stop, in the school. And Dad? That night I told him the story.

"You did what?"

"I did what you said, Dad, hit the guy, smashed him on the head."

"I told you to do that?" He struggled to remember the off-handed comment he had made the night before.

"Ah, yeah," I said.

Dad smiled, and put his hand on my shoulder.

"David, it looks like you got things straightened out with that kid, but do me a favor. Don't do everything I tell you, okay?"

He laughed and pretend-punched me on the arm. It may have been the first time I realized Dad wasn't always going to be right, and maybe I could be wrong, too, sometimes. But it also wasn't the first and certainly not the last time Dad would help me realize I could handle anything, anyone, anytime. I could stand on my own.

As I faced my new life as a student, teacher, and a single dad, my father confronted doctors and medical reports. A blip in a routine test showed cancer of the prostate. The experts told us, at sixty-eight, Dad would likely die of old age before the slow-moving cancer got him. Still, I checked in by phone regularly, anxious about the most recent news from the doctors' offices. The reports were troubling.

"Hello," Dad said with forced vibrato, trying to protect me from the bad news. I had already spoken with Mom and been briefed on the rough details, the cold statistics of the latest test results.

"Hey, Norm," I said. I had called my father by his first name for some time, starting years earlier as a joke, then becoming our shared sign of affection. "So, the doctor had a few things to say, huh." I found myself trying to soften the real truth, real feelings.

"Yeah, not so good, Dave, not so good." He immediately abandoned the positive tone. "My PSA number is up, my legs are aching more, and I keep losing weight, another five pounds, Dave. Another five pounds."

Dad was dying. I knew it, he knew it, and it changed everything.

Chapter 5

The voice crackled through the tiny, rusted-out speaker on the outside door.

"Can I help you?"

It was one of those intercom systems used for security. The front entrance to Cowherd Middle School was locked, and the electronic push-to-talk button was the only way to alert anyone of your presence. I pressed it four times before anyone responded.

"I'm here for the orientation?"

Nothing. I waited.

Orientation for new teachers began at East Aurora High School on a hot day in the early summer. Dutifully, dozens of us marched into the aging school on the south side of town in a cruelly battered neighborhood. The new hires sat through mindless seminars inside the tired classrooms, then split up and headed to the schools where each would teach. I would go inside Cowherd for the first time.

The glass doors had what appeared to be permanent smudges on them; there were chips out of the side glass panels, blemishes left from someone throwing stones. A screechy buzzer signaled an open door and permission to enter, but there was only a moment to pull the door before it locked again. I was just quick enough.

"Hi, I'm Terri," said the woman who would be our guide to the school. "We're waiting for two others."

Her words were terse; she offered only an obligatory smile and made no small talk. She definitely hadn't volunteered for the job.

Once inside, the odor was unavoidable—sourness from the overload of bodies, a hint of cleaning solution, the stale smell of a building built with concrete blocks, an institution, a fortress. The fluorescent lighting was excessively bright like the hallways of a hospital.

In about two minutes, the others arrived. It felt like two hours.

"Where's the closest place to get a beer around here?" Carly was one of the three new teachers, myself included, scheduled for this mandatory walk-through at Cowherd. She was a striking woman in her early thirties, a looker with sharp features and soft brown hair to her shoulders. For such a young age, she seemed curiously hardened to the teaching profession, and her questions to our Cowherd host were almost urgent. "Where does everyone go on Friday nights after the kids are gone?"

Carly said she had bounced around teaching classes in a number of Chicago suburbs, including a little time spent in the nearby affluent Naperville school district, just a few miles from Aurora. She was brash, but likable, and being double-take pretty didn't hurt. But I wondered what kind of teacher asks about where to get a beer on her first day on the job?

Tom was the other new teacher, a short, fireplug kind of guy. He was part of a construction crew over the summer months and it showed; fullback muscles filled up his blue jeans and striped dress shirt. Cowherd was his first teaching gig out of college, and that brought with it a blind confidence and a natural enthusiasm that youth's inherent idealism nearly always breeds. But on this day, his enthusiasm was directed at Carly.

His eyes moved over her like searchlights.

"Are you old enough to drink?" he asked, with the skill of someone who had spent his share of evenings in taverns built for the young and single. A corny line, but it got him a smile. I felt old.

Terri, our guide, had been teaching at Cowherd for a few years. She also was young, somewhere in age between Carly and Tom, and was familiar with the school's labyrinth layout, the frequent and seemingly erratic administrative changes, the people to remember, the people to forget, and the ones to avoid.

"As you know, it's up to you to make this place what you want it to be," she said, as if reading from the Cowherd play-book and at the same time revealing the school's reputation. "It's up to you to decide whether this will be a good or bad experience."

That was all she said about teaching, the job, the students. The rest was simply cold, logistical detail. "Here's the bathroom, the mailboxes, that's the gym. The doors are locked all day, every door. Security issue." There was no embellishment, no emotion, like Detective Joe Friday from TV's *Dragnet*—"Just the facts, ma'am."

We asked about incidents, rumors others had told us—the regular drug sweeps, the story of the eighth grade girl selling herself in the bathrooms for CD money. Terri volunteered no insight into any of it. And what about the former Cowherd principal who apparently walked out in the middle of the day because she couldn't take it anymore? Terri claimed to know nothing about it. We didn't know what to believe.

"What's the story on the kid with the gun? I heard someone brought in a gun," Carly asked.

"Gun?" Terri said, searching her memory and not at all flustered by the blunt question. "Well, I've heard gun stories, too, but honestly, it's just that, talk. People hear a lot."

It seemed gun stories surfaced every few weeks. It was part of the landscape. Nothing new, and nearly impossible to verify.

Terri seamlessly changed subjects.

"Paydays come twice a month. If you substitute during your prep-period, be sure to put in for it. You get a small stipend."

The Cowherd orientation lasted less than a half hour, and afterward we were free to go home. In just a few days, I would be back.

When I was twenty years old, in my undergraduate days at Clarion University, a state school tucked in the mountains of middle Pennsylvania, I believed I had everything figured out. I was convinced that the music I played and the songs I tried to write with my scratched-up acoustic Yamaha guitar were the melodies of my life. I filled my hours with music, creating it, listening to it, playing it on the turntables of the student radio station. My literary diet was Kerouac, Thoreau, and Hunter S. Thompson. I subscribed to *Rolling Stone*, wore a denim jacket with a Woodstock patch on the sleeve. I protested tuition hikes by marching to the university president's campus residence (the Vietnam War was over and I itched to protest something), I smoked Marlboro Lights—bumming them from college buddies who puffed more than I did—and spent hundreds of hours with friends over cold cups of diner coffee, talking about how we would change the world.

But nothing stays the same. Not the idealism of my youth, not my marriage, not the business I thought I loved.

The artistic creation, the free-spiritedness of my college and early radio days ultimately were dismissed in the bottom-line, corporate life of broadcasting. It was no longer about the music or the messages revealed and discovered on free-form stations with air personalities who believed the rants and rhythms of the day could make a difference. Radio station owners discovered if they used a business model instead of an artistic model, radio could make them rich. So, over time, without consciously knowing it, I compromised, too. I sold out. I suppressed my passions and was swept up in the industry's new corporate structure. The hippie morphed into a yuppie.

But maybe now it could be different. Maybe in spirit, I

could return to those old days. Maybe there was something in the classroom, in teaching, that would shake to the surface the sparks that fueled me in my twenties.

In the heart of the summer, I went through a practicum, a practice period during the summer school session. It was my first time in the classroom at Cowherd, and I wanted to make an impression. It was day one when I started wearing the tie.

"Got a pair of scissors, anyone?" Her name was Jenny, a female teacher built like an offensive lineman, who ran her classroom with tough love. She was also a drill sergeant, my drill sergeant. Jenny was hired to train me, whip me into shape, babysit me during the practicum, and she was known to ride the newbies any chance she could.

"We'll get rid of that thing quick enough," she said, making the two-fingered hand signal for working shears just inches from my tightly dimpled knot.

The tie proved to be the center of attention, evoking a few giggles. Most every teacher and administrator dressed as if they were heading for a picnic at summer camp—shorts, T-shirts, even sandals. Formality was frowned on at Cowherd, and all I was trying to do was take my new job seriously. I had apparently watched too many TV shows, movies, where the professorially dressed teacher wore a tweed jacket, khaki pants, and, yes, a tie. Think *To Sir with Love, Dead Poets Society*, even *Welcome Back, Kotter*. I knew enough to skip the coat and khakis, but not the tie.

There were ten students in our classroom, nearly all Hispanic, most Mexican, and one African-American girl. On the first morning of the first summer school day, my welcome was far from enthusiastic.

"This is Mr. Berner," Jenny said. "He'll be working with us this summer."

Who the hell cares? That's what they were thinking. They looked me over, judged me, like I had just walked into the wrong neighborhood. *Do you know where you are, whitey? Go home. You're just going to be like the rest, and we really don't want to hear what you have to say, what you're going to do, or anything about you.*

These were thirteen- and fourteen-year-olds—shouldn't there be some sense of childlike happiness, a light heart? I knew they didn't want to be in summer school, but still, they were kids. Where was the innate joy? Instead, defiance was before me—an arms-crossed, I-dare-you attitude. One girl, with an inch-long scar across her forehead, refused to take her eyes off me, as if she were stalking prey. A boy in the back row, wearing a white T-shirt and visible tattoos down his right arm, nervously hit his fists on the desk, drumming out a musical rhythm with the middle fingers of each hand stretched out from the others. A subtle, indirect "fuck you." Some put their heads on the desks and slept. Others looked out the window, wishing themselves on the other side of the glass. Every one of these students was in danger of failing, some for academic reasons, some for disciplinary reasons. I would be with them four days a week, five hours a day.

I sat in the back of the class observing for a few days, as Jenny had instructed, sizing up some of the kids the best I could, trying to make even minor connections with them. Most of the time it seemed pointless. But during the second week, one student got curious.

"Where do you live, mister?" he said, trying to determine if I was from his side of town. I'm sure he already knew I wasn't.

"Ricky, I live in Naperville, a few miles from here."

It was as if he needed to confirm his distrust and validate his reasons for dismissing me. Ricky nodded his head slightly, paused, and asked another question.

"You married?"

"I have two boys," I answered, trying to avoid the issue.

"How old? They play baseball?"

"Yep, they both play. I'm coaching their team."

"I play, too," he said, offering me the first glimpse of his life outside the classroom. "Couple home runs already this year. And, by the way," he continued, pausing and leaning back in his chair as if to allow what he had to say next to be more easily heard by others, "what's with the tie?"

I'm not sure why Ricky opened up. It was brave of him to question me when the others in the class appeared to want no part of me. I tried not to overanalyze it, and instead made it a point to keep the communication going, talking baseball as often as we could. We talked at recess, during breaks, before and after school. Then it hit me. Could I use baseball to help Ricky get through summer session? Could it be a writing topic? Could he read books about baseball?

"I can't stand school," Ricky would say. "I just want to play ball."

Maybe I was on to something.

"You want to come to one of my games?" Ricky asked during one of the lunch breaks. The question surprised me. It was a level of acceptance I wasn't completely ready for, and I didn't know quite how to respond. I wonder why I didn't just simply say, "I'd be glad to." Why wasn't that the natural reaction? Was I tentative about this relationship, a *real* relationship with any of these kids? Like many of them, I wasn't comfortable yet with the unique, sometimes delicate interplay between student and teacher, especially in this district.

School counselors told me Cowherd's boys were starved for father figures. Fathers, many times, were not living at home and rarely a part of their children's lives, or the fathers worked so much, manual labor jobs to make ends meet, they were never around to have an impact. I was a commodity. In a middle school environment like this one, I was rare—a male teacher, a symbol of male commitment to young teenage boys. I thought about my father and my own young teenage years. What would they have been like without him?

"When do you play, Ricky? What days of the week?"

"I have a game tonight," he said, quickly.

"Ricky, you get me a schedule, I'll take a look at it and I'll get there one of these nights. Maybe, I'll even bring my sons."

"Really? You would come to my game?"

I surprised myself with my response, coming out of my mouth as if I had no control, a visceral reaction.

"Sure I would. It'd be fun. What position do you play?"

We discussed Ricky's hitting record, his team's strengths and weaknesses, my sons' team, the Cubs, and Sammy Sosa, Chicago's power hitter of the day. This time the baseball talk was different, animated and passionate.

The next week, I took my son and one of his friends to Ricky's game at a ball field deep behind the small homes in the Hispanic neighborhood just a quarter-mile from Cowherd. We were the only whites anywhere.

"Boy, this is not Naperville. Kind of ghetto," said my son's friend.

"Like the city," added Casey.

The boys were much like me at their age. The issues of race and economic status were only intellectual, something you heard or read about, but rarely experienced. I felt good about bringing Casey along, showing him another side of life, and a little glimpse at Dad's new career. I hoped Casey would recognize his father was doing something meaningful and that I wanted to share it.

Ricky was in the dugout when we arrived at the ballpark, a dusty diamond set back behind several frame homes. The field was in better shape than I expected, and the teams even had benches to sit on in their dugouts.

"Ricky." I tried to get his attention. "Ricky," I said again, this time a bit louder with my hands cupped around my mouth.

From the home team bench, he turned my way and gave a tentative wave.

"When are you up?" I said.

"Hey, Mr. Berner. Pretty soon," he said, standing to get closer to the fence.

My son and his friend moved down the third base line to watch the game. I stayed closer to the dugout.

Ricky was in a black hat, his dark hair falling out of the sides and back. He wore a black and white baseball uniform that appeared to have seen better years. In the four-tiered stands were a few parents and friends, with some teenage boys and girls scattered around enjoying the clear and warm summer evening.

Ricky came around the fencing. I shook his hand. "How's the game going?" I asked.

"We're up by two," Ricky said. "Is that your son down there?"

"Yep, that's Casey and his friend Jimmy."

Ricky took a moment to watch them, as if to be sure of whom they were and how they fit into my life, his, and this night.

"I got to get back," Ricky said, moving toward his teammates to grab a bat and put on his helmet. "I'm up soon. How long you staying?"

"We'll be here, Ricky. We won't miss you."

Behind the backstop at home plate, small groups of kids and teens, family and friends sat or stood. Few were actually watching the game; instead they talked and laughed, glancing now and then at the diamond. When a batter made ball contact, most would look up to see the results—some clapped, hooted, or hollered at the players.

Ricky was a righty and stood big in the box, a giant next to his teammates, tall and a bit overweight in a way that suggested when he wasn't playing baseball he probably was watching TV. The ill-fitting uniform made him look even bigger.

"Knock it long, Ricky," I yelled.

He gave me a glance over his shoulder.

Strike one. Ricky took a big cut, fanning the air and twisting his body out of balance.

Strike two. He turned to look at the umpire, showing disapproval, just like a major leaguer.

Hands clapped. Shouts came from the bench, the stands.

"Andale, Ricky. Pégale a la pelota!"

"Pégale a la pelota! Andale!"

The pitcher wasted no time. He locked eyes with the catcher, placed his foot on the rubber, moved gracefully into his wind-up, then hurled his whole body toward Ricky. The ball pierced the air. For a second, there was a hush. If you know the game, you know the unique stillness that comes just at the pinnacle of pent-up, tightly wound tension.

Ricky's body leaned toward the catcher, as if loading up the power he possessed. His bat twitched above his right shoulder. The ball came in at the belt level, and Ricky's arms stretched out to force wood against stitched leather. The sound of the collision was unmistakable—a sharp, violent crack—and in a blur the ball, flying inches above the ground, tore down the third base line, past a diving infielder and into the outfield. Ricky chugged his way to first, his cap falling from his head. He could hit, but no one would say Ricky had speed. After rounding first and electing to settle with a single, he stood on the bag and glanced my way, a shy smile on his face.

The inning produced nothing. Ricky was stranded at first. After grabbing his glove to head back on the field, Ricky came back around the other side of the fence.

"Pretty good rip, huh?"

"Nice hit, Ricky, way to go. Hey, where are your parents?" I asked this reluctantly, not wanting to draw attention to their absence if they didn't attend.

"Standing over there," Ricky said, pointing to the third base fence about a hundred feet away. His father wore a white T-shirt, blue jeans, and a worn baseball cap. He appeared as if he had just come off a construction or landscaping job site. His mother was dressed modestly in a colorful sundress and held a young girl in her arms, Ricky's sister.

"I want to meet them. Will you introduce me?"

"Yeah, okay," he said without much commitment to the idea and no immediate move to actually do it. Ricky headed back onto the field.

After a couple of innings, I said hello on my own.

"Inglés?" I asked.

"Un poco," his mother said, smiling nervously.

"I'm Ricky's teacher, Mr. Berner."

His father reached out his hand to shake mine. His mother nodded, smiled shyly, directing her eyes to the ground.

Through their broken English and my rudimentary Spanish we were able to communicate a bit. I told them Ricky had asked me to come to the game, that I liked their son, and that he talked about baseball a lot at school.

"Si," he said, smiling and acknowledging Ricky's passion. *"Alway bay-ball, alway."*

I shook their hands, said good-bye, telling them I was honored to meet them. I then turned to seek out Ricky. From the dugout, his eyes met mine immediately. He had been watching my exchange with his parents. Ricky gave me a simple, waist-high wave, and I smiled back.

I stayed another half hour or so, then called out to Ricky.

"Got to go, buddy. See you in class."

He lumbered over from the dugout.

"Thanks for coming," he said. It took a lot for him to thank me, to thank anyone.

"It was great."

As the boys and I headed back to the car, up the cracked cement steps to the gravel parking lot, I heard cheers coming from the field behind us.

"Maybe Ricky got another hit, Dad," Casey said.

I stood on the small hill in front of the parking lot for a moment, my hands in my pockets, my eyes toward the diamond.

"Yeah, maybe," I said. "And tomorrow, I'm sure he'll tell me all about it."

Chapter 6

Part of the teaching job in the summer session was to formally test students on their reading ability. Jenny warned me, "The scores are going to be poor—really bad." But, I never expected to see the kinds of results we found. Nearly every one of the soon-to-be eighth grade students was reading at second or, at best, third grade level. They routinely struggled to get through simple declarative sentences.

"The...the boy, walked...walked down the..."

"Boulevard," I said as I tried to help a student through a reading exercise. His name was Carlos. "The word is *boulevard*. Do you know what that means?"

"Bull-a-what?" he said.

"It's like a street, but fancier," I said. "*Boulevard*."

"He stopped...to, to talk...with...the workers, workers like..." Carlos then looked up from the page, pointing to a word. "What's this?"

Carlos had never seen the word *plumber* before. He certainly had heard it, but not read it, seen it in print.

"Oh, okay, a *plumber*," he said. "Why is there a 'b' in the word?"

"Good question, Carlos. Good question."

Part of the difficulty was language itself. Many of the students spoke only Spanish at home. English was what students called "school language," and that created a kind of barrier between their home lives and their school lives. Plus, there were cultural and social differences. Many families raised their children in the traditions of the migrant laborers, where work and family came first, education was a distant third, and books were rarely part of life at home. Illiterate parents seemed to place little value in reading, and for many of the students, reading a book was what was done at school, and only school. The children's bookshelf I had in my home as a child, and the ones my children had in their bedrooms, apparently didn't exist in the homes of Cowherd's students.

I thought about all those nights I sat beside my sons' beds or crawled in with them to cuddle up with a Dr. Seuss book or their favorite, *Goodnight Moon*. My mother had done the same with me. But my most memorable book was *Go, Dogs, Go* by P.D. Eastman. It was filled with Seuss-like rhymes and bright, colorful cartoon drawings of all kinds of dogs—tiny dogs and enormous ones, ones with big noses and small tails, yellow and red and even blue dogs.

"Look at the dogs in the bed," my mother said, as we read it together, both of us laughing at the silliness of the drawing. Dozens of dogs, a crayon box of colors, huddled in an oversized bed, the covers pulled up, their ears and paws flopping over one another, each with their eyes closed. Except for one.

"Mom, that dog's eyes are so big," I said, giggling. "He looks like he can't sleep or he's scared or maybe he heard something."

"Oh," she said, giggling right along with me. "I think he's thinking about something. Maybe food, or a bone. His mind must be so busy, don't you think?"

As I grew older, even into my young teenage years when my reading expanded onto *Black Beauty* and *Lassie Come Home* and books about Babe Ruth, and Roberto Clemente, and the Beatles, I still would pick up *Go, Dogs, Go* and read it with my mother, still laugh, still wonder what the dog with the big eyes was thinking.

The summer gave me a chance to teach a few lessons with Jenny guiding the way. We became a pretty good team, I thought, a one-act reality play starring the veteran and the rookie—Jenny, in her shorts and T-shirt, and me in my Windsor knot.

And near the end of the summer session, Jenny gave me a challenge.

"I want you to design your own lesson for tomorrow. All yours. No help from me," she said.

I was ready. In fact, I thought I was ready weeks before. Confidence had been building.

The lesson was to develop in-class student newspapers.

The students worked in groups, choosing stories and ideas, cartoons, and advertising from copies of real newspapers. They had to give each edition a name and physically develop the front page with construction paper, crayons, paint, stencils, glue, and story clippings. The project was a twist on a lesson plan I had read in a graduate school textbook. The original involved computers, but that wasn't going to happen at Cowherd. There was a computer lab in the school, but the computers were ten years old, many frequently crashed, and each was locked from Internet access with a series of passwords so the students couldn't get to the porn sites. Booting them up and getting them running was many times more work than it was worth.

The goal of the lesson was to build an interest in a wide range of subjects, issues relevant to their age group. Hopefully it would begin to motivate them to have a keener sense of the world around them. Plus, there was the reading component. Students would have to read what they chose before putting it in their newspapers. It all seemed pedagogically sound. At least that's what I thought.

"Fuck you, that sucks," one student snapped, arguing over the use of red construction paper.

"Shut up, faggot." That reply came as one student nailed

another in the head with a flying Goldenrod Crayola.

The lesson quickly deteriorated into a chaotic craft project, a glue fight, a crayon-breaking contest, peppered with biting exchanges.

"Hey, guys. It's all right to argue, to disagree," I said, trying my best to hose down the language. "But let's try to do it with some respect, okay?"

After saying this, or something like it, several times over, I eventually was able to get most of the kids reasonably focused. After about an hour, there was tangible progress, and the newspapers started to emerge with bold student-chosen headlines:

Aurora Drug Bust, Two Arrested

Cubs Win

Christina Aguilera Has a New CD

And since teenage boys were involved in the project, advertisements of a certain specific type appeared prominently in the papers:

Bra Sale at Marshall Fields

Bare-Assets Gentleman's Club

Viagra Can Save Your Sex Life

Despite the rough start, in the end I figured I made some points—with the kids, and the teacher.

"That seemed to work," said Jenny during a break between creating the newspapers and the kids' presentations. During the lesson, she had sat quietly in the back of the room, saying nothing, refraining from intervening. "I did see them get over on you, though."

Get over on me? When? Where? Who? I never saw that. Sure, rocky at the start, but I thought I was able to gain pretty solid control. I thought I used an effective mix of strictness, humor, openness, and restraint.

"You were a little too nice, tried to be their buddy. Good lesson. Most of them got something out of it. But, these kids, you can't always be their friend. They'll use you. They'll squeeze what they want out of you, and leave the learning in the dust," Jenny said.

I wanted an example.

"Carlos, for instance. The only work he really did was cut out the strip club ads from the paper. Does that mean he got something out of the lesson? Oh sure, he worked with the group, but not as well as he could have. You have to monitor these kids constantly, and you did. But massaging them mentally, redirecting them continually is an absolute necessity and the hardest part of the job."

Carlos was a tough kid, a big strong football player with a buzz cut. He had problems at home with other family members who were involved in drugs and gangs. So far, Carlos was keeping out of trouble.

"When it comes to school work, don't be easy on Carlos," said Jenny. "He can be shy sometimes, and he may need a gentle touch outside of the classroom. But in class, you got to ride him. He can handle it."

What the students learned that day was not as important as what I learned—good teachers know their students, really know them, each of them, incredibly well. They know family life, nuances in personalities, and what might motivate each individual kid. It might seem a simple lesson, but at that stage of my teaching life, it was an awakening. I had connected with Ricky, but I had to do the same with others, and I had to do it over and over and over.

"Hey, what's your name again?" asked one student during a break in the academic day. We took students outside for some fresh air. Keeping them inside all day, without a little free time, wore the students down, wore teachers down. We all needed time to stretch, and get our heads out of the books.

"Mr. Berner," I said, tossing the basketball to Carlos. "Let's play some hoops, guys."

"You're going to play with us?" Carlos said with disbelief and sarcasm, as if I was making a joke.

"Yeah, sure. Don't you think I can handle it?"

"Hey, man, you're a dude. Tie and all. Bald. You're already sweating."

It was certainly cooler in the classroom despite the inefficiencies of the clunky, oversized window air conditioner. But getting the kids outside for a time was necessary, even if it was ninety degrees, even if heat waves rose off the pockmarked concrete court.

I tucked the long end of my tie into my shirt and rolled up my sleeves.

"Let's see the ball," I said, looking at Carlos.

I took a shot and made a fifteen-footer. No one said a word. One student chased down the ball and dribbled it to the foul line. He turned, fired, and made it. I fumbled for the rebound, dribbled, and passed it to another student.

"Hey, man, you can't just pass it like that," one of them said. "We never made teams or anything. Shit, man, get it together."

"All right, let's make teams," I said.

But no one made an effort to do any such thing. The group of five boys just kept shooting, dribbling, and shooting again. There was no sport to this. It was simply get the ball, be selfish, take a shot, and if you made it, prance around like an arrogant NBA player. So, I joined in—shooting, dribbling, shooting again, and, when I made it, a little prancing.

No one talked. The only sound was the rhythmic snap of the ball against concrete and the clang as it collided with the metal backstop. The frantic shooting kept up for ten minutes, plenty of time to realize how out of shape I was.

"Okay, guys, let's go," Jenny yelled from across the shady side of the court. "Wrap it up."

There were a few more shots, attempts to prolong the outdoor break.

"Now, guys," Jenny said, sternly.

I wiped the sweat from my forehead and the back of my neck, and helped to direct the students to the side door and back inside.

"Hey, you gonna play again tomorrow, mister?" Carlos asked while tossing the basketball back and forth, chest high, between his right and left hand.

"Yeah, yeah," I said, breathlessly, not expecting to be asked that question. "It's the last day tomorrow, ya know?"

"Really? Well, you can still play hoops, right?"

"You bet, Carlos. Yeah, you bet."

A little sweaty game of basketball may have opened a few doors.

It was weeks later, we had managed to get the summer students onto eighth grade—Ricky and Carlos included—and my focus now was on the start of the official school year. I had been arriving early, just a few minutes before 7:00 a.m., getting a jump on the day and the fall semester, sharing the hours just after dawn with only one other school employee—the janitor. But on one particular morning, we were not alone.

As I walked past the copy machine in the room behind the main office and toward the supply closet, I saw the backs of a man and two women, each facing an open supply closet door, stuffing plastic garbage bags with index cards, crayons, highlighters, you name it.

"You the new guy?" one asked, snapping her head to look over her shoulder at me, then quickly returning to the job at hand. Her name was Sandra, a three-year veteran and one of the few African-American teachers.

"Yeah, Dave Berner. Hello."

"Hey," said Bill, his back to me as he rifled handfuls of paper tablets into his bag. Bill was a seventh grade teacher.

"Get your stuff yet?" said Joanna, the younger of the two female teachers, glancing only momentarily at me, then back to the closet where her hands reached in to snatch boxes of paperclips. "It'll be gone soon. Maybe today."

They all laughed.

"Maybe this morning," said Bill.

More laughter.

"Don't wait, get it now, or you'll run out, have nothing," said Sandra, keeping up a rhythm of grab and stash, grab and stash.

"Yeah, okay," I said, hesitating. "Is this the only closet?"

"This is it, man," Bill said. "Go for it."

I reluctantly nudged my way between Joanna and Bill and

started stacking supplies in my arms, making a point to reach for the last box of pencils.

Covert operations were officially underway; plenty of jockeying for what little was available. It was part of the Cowherd experience to grab what you needed before supplies ran out. If you didn't, you would be digging into your own wallet to buy paper, folders, tablets, pens, crayons, markers, blackboard erasers, and yes, pencils. Wal-Mart became a regular stop for me. I knew the greeters by name.

It was also good to get to know Enrique.

He had been the janitor at the school for as long as anyone could remember. Dressed in his olive green uniform, usually with a screwdriver or wrench in his hand, Enrique was quick to tell you what he could do for you—fix a window, change a lock, repair a light switch, hang a map of the U.S. in your classroom. He cleaned, he moved desks and cabinets, he emptied garbage, and kept the toilets flushing. He was there when you arrived in the morning, and there when you left.

"Got what you need?" Enrique would ask.

"All set." I nearly always said I had what I needed, even if I didn't. Burdening Enrique with another issue or another question when he was already so busy seemed almost cruel. But I knew if you had a question, he usually had the answer. And I certainly had plenty of questions for anyone who would listen. Where were the administrators? What about textbooks? Was I to teach language arts only? Was there a curriculum I should be studying? Lesson plans, what about them? I still hadn't spoken to a school administrator about my specific assignment at Cowherd, and still hadn't met the principal. And what about the students? How many would I have? How many classes? Was there a teachers' cafeteria? Would I have lunch duty? What am I exactly getting paid? And, while you're at it, can you answer a few questions about my new life as a grad student, my dying father, and my divorce?

In my hands I balanced a cardboard box filled with all the stuff I had snatched out of the supply closet.

"Got what you need?" Enrique asked as he passed me

walking down the main hallway toward the school's main door and out to the parking lot.

"Got it, Enrique," I said. "But let me ask you something. By chance, do you know my room number?"

"Can't help you there, Mr. Berner," said Enrique, looking at my box of supplies. "You don't want to put that stuff in your room, anyway. Someone's bound to steal it, ya know." He winked at me, smiled, and held the front door so I could squeeze out into the late afternoon sun.

"Enrique, do teachers really do that?"

A moment passed and he smiled again.

"Have a good night, Mr. Berner. See you tomorrow."

The summer may have given me a better handle on the students, but I still had other lessons to learn.

Chapter 7

I think there were times when Martin truly believed his life was in danger.

"They have no respect for anything, anywhere, anytime," he said, the rush of blood reddening his face as he told his story. "These students come to class looking, acting like they are ready to fight. They're angry. They look like they want to beat me up, kill someone. And I'm supposed to teach them something?"

Martin came to the graduate cohort class, the last of the summer, edgy and tormented. I wouldn't have been surprised if he had announced he was ready to quit the program.

"I just don't know about this. I just don't know."

The grad class was designed so we could share our summer teaching experiences, and although each of us had something to say, it was obvious Martin needed to talk more than anyone else.

"Is this really worth it? Right now, I'm not sure."

Martin was a middle-aged white guy, about my age, but appeared ten years older. He wore oversized, out-of-date glasses. His clothes looked like they came off the racks at Sears, his shoes from K-Mart; he wasn't cheap, he was frugal. This soft-spoken man was being destroyed in the summer classroom at East Aurora High School, where students could be rude, crude, threatening, even violent, and could lock their sights on your Achilles heel from the far end of a school hallway.

The cohort had lost a few people over the summer. Some had left because of other job offers, personal reasons, and some just disappeared from the program. But a core of us kept on. It was an eclectic bunch—two or three from the accounting world, a sales associate, a couple of former teaching substitutes, a young man freshly discharged from the army, a woman recently divorced with a young child and living with her parents, me, the old reporter, and even the African-American daughter of the former administrator of the East Aurora School District. Nora had recently left the corporate recruiting business with the itch to teach. She was outspoken, blunt, and some called her abrasive.

"Martin, get it together, man," Nora said, looking him directly in the eye. "You can't be so straight, so stiff. You tend to be rigid in what you think is right. These kids are not like you, Martin. You better realize it quick or it's gonna get ugly."

"It's already ugly. But it's not me. It's them. They tell me to go 'get fucked,' right in the middle of class, right out loud. Can you believe that?"

Martin and Nora had very different philosophies about teaching in a rough-and-tumble district, different thoughts on most everything—politics, religion, how to raise children. But despite this, the cohort members had rapidly developed a working camaraderie, and we sympathized, if not empathized, with Martin's experiences. We also embraced the incredible importance of time. What would get each of us through the rough periods would be perseverance, surviving each day. The cohort eventually helped Martin realize this, and he remained in the program, became a solid teacher. But, in moments alone, we all thanked God that Martin's tumultuous summer teaching experience had not been ours.

The faculty lunchroom at Cowherd, a small, windowless

space, smelled like a dormitory laundry room—a mix of Tide and old socks. The cheeseburger on my plate appeared to be a warmed-up leftover, the fries soggy and colorless, almost translucent.

"So, you settling in yet?" asked a burly and brash phys-ed instructor who had been at Cowherd for several years. He was one of three teachers, myself included, grabbing a bite from the school cafeteria during one of the last teacher in-service days before the students returned for the fall.

"I was here during the summer, but I'm still not sure about the details of my assignment. I still haven't met the principal."

"Principal?" He laughed. "You wouldn't expect us to have a principal just a couple of days before school starts, would you?"

I smiled, accepting his sarcasm.

"The other one quit, ya know, so we're waiting to meet the next. They better hurry the hell up, don't you think?" he said, shaking his head. "Jesus, this place."

"Yeah, nice to have the principal before the little fuckers show up," said the only other teacher in the lunchroom, a thin, bespectacled math instructor in her forties, with a 1980s hairstyle and a plaid skirt. Not the type you would have expected to say "fuckers."

It appeared the job of a Cowherd teacher, I quickly learned, was simply to get these kids out the door and into high school without hurting themselves and without losing your mind. Sure, there was talk about teaching strategy and motivation, discussions about multiple intelligences (the different ways people learn) and developing better lesson plans. But most of the time, teachers talked about discipline, about the dozens of daily referrals they wrote to the assistant principal documenting disrespect, defiance, fights. And maybe, more than anything else, many of the teachers talked about how they hated their jobs.

I tried to change the subject.

"So, any hope for the Bears this season?"

This is the moment when I realized how green I was. As much as I thought I might have been different, I was instead very much the same as every new teacher—full of ideas, hope, and idealism, ready to change the world one student at a time, but incredibly, sadly naïve.

"They're gonna suck," the gym teacher said, as he flipped his half-eaten burger into the trash and tossed his lunch tray on the counter. "See you around the plant," he said, walking out into the hallway.

I dipped a fry into catsup, hoping to make it edible.

"Where were you before Cowherd?" the math teacher asked, sipping from her plastic cup filled with ice and Coke.

"First time teaching," I said. "New career."

"Oh. Really. One of *those*." She put her glass to her mouth again, keeping her eyes on me.

"It's a university program to transition those with other careers into teaching. Heard of it?" I asked, in the nicest way I knew how and at the same time trying to justify my job.

"Oh, yeah, I've heard of it." She took a final drink and dumped the remainder of ice and cola in the trash.

"You know," she said, wiping her hands with a napkin, "your job was to be filled by an experienced teacher. There were several who are on strike in another district, and they applied for your job."

"Really," I said, feeling my defenses go up.

"You aren't even certified yet. You haven't paid your dues. Nothing against you personally, but the whole thing is crap."

Technically, as part of the program, I was working at Cowherd as a paid intern. Certification wouldn't come until I received my graduate degree. And, she was right; there were a lot of experienced teachers looking for work.

"This is where I was assigned. I'm just trying to get through the program, do the best I can."

"Yeah, yeah, I know, I understand," she said. "But it still pisses me off."

She placed her now empty cup on the counter, partially opened the door to the hall, and paused a moment.

"Who's your team leader?"

"Mrs. Murray, eighth grade."

"That's good. She's good."

There was an uncomfortable quiet, a few seconds of suspended time.

"You'll be fine. Don't worry about it," she said, stepping through the door, leaving me alone in the lunchroom.

"Thanks, appreciate it," I said, my words coming too late for her to hear them. She was already gone.

In just a few days nearly a thousand students would march into Cowherd, over three hundred of them would be eighth graders, about one hundred and fifty of them would be part of my team, and some twenty students would be seated at the desks in Room 108 for the first period class. And only one teacher would stand before them, all by himself.

Chapter 8

When I was a full-time journalist, a cup of Starbucks was my usual morning brew. It seemed an appropriate companion—carrying around the white paper cup with the brown recyclable sleeve, along with my recorder and notepad. But as a teacher in one of the most economically strained districts in Illinois, a double-shot skim latte seemed far out of place.

I switched to Dunkin' Donuts.

Coffee from Dunkin'—light cream, one Equal—was in my hand as I walked through Cowherd's doors each morning. I'd sip from the white and red Styrofoam cup through first period, and routinely leave just a taste to turn cold on my classroom desk. The students rarely brought drinks into school in the morning, but they did bring breakfast. Pop-Tarts, Twinkies, and any other variety of plastic-sealed convenience store junk food, even bags of popcorn were routinely found in their hands just outside the classroom doors before the start of the day. So, for one student to be offering little pieces of chocolate to others in the hallway just seemed like part of the daily morning menu. I was offered a piece, but declined. That turned out to be a smart move.

The first three weeks of school were behind me. I met each of the teachers on my eighth grade team, seemed to be getting to know the students' names and faces, and slowly was finding some minor comfort in daily routines. But on this morning, I was looking forward to a bit of a diversion from the usual day.

Carol, our new principal, had planned a school assembly in the gymnasium honoring students who had done well academically the previous school year. Mrs. Goodman, as the students called her, was already aggressively trying to set a new tone around the place. There was a bit of old hippie in her personality, believing "everyone could find their purpose, themselves, find their own way." Plus, she had that earthy look—denim skirt, Joni Mitchell's hair, John Lennon's wire-rimmed glasses.

Students filed into the gym and took their seats on the wooden bleachers while the honor students sat in foldout metal chairs on the hardwood basketball floor. Those who received As at Cowherd would likely get Cs at most other junior high schools in the state. All I had to do was compare what was being taught at Cowherd with what my own sons were learning. Still, Carol insisted on acknowledging students with good grades, apparently hoping it would motivate the others.

It was just as the assembly began that hands rose into the air.

"Mr. Berner," the young girl in the group of honorees whispered after I recognized her raised hand. "I have to go to the bathroom."

I excused her and turned to take my place against the wall with the other teachers.

Another hand went up.

"I think I need to go, too," another girl said softly as the principal began to address the crowd.

I hesitated somewhat to let her go after being burned a couple days before when a bunch of girls in different classrooms coordinated a scheme to be dismissed at the exact same time so they could meet in the bathroom to smoke. But, this girl had a desperate, please-don't-let-me-wait look.

It was then that one of the dean's assistants came through the gym doors and leaned in with some news.

"Thought I'd let you know," he whispered. "Apparently one of the kids has been passing out Exlax. The chocolate-favored stuff. And the kids have been eating it. Lots of it. They think it's candy."

I remembered the chocolate in the hall before first period.

I turned to look back at the students. Two more hands stretched skyward.

"Some kids ate three or four pieces. Maybe more," the assistant added.

I watched as yet another hand reached above another head.

Does Exlax really do that? Aren't these kinds of immediate effects on the digestive tract some kind of urban myth?

One more hand rose into the air.

This is like the script from a very bad teen movie, the scene where the school jocks pull off some wacky prank against the geeks.

Could this be some sort of elaborate plan by some of the kids to disrupt things? Is this really the way a laxative works?

"Can we really believe what's going on here?" I asked the assistant dean after giving permission to another student to head for the restroom.

"Do you want to be the one to say 'no' to a kid who really needs to go?" he said. "Maybe *you*, but not *me*."

Good point.

Eventually, at least a dozen kids were dismissed during the first five minutes of the assembly, and a couple more as the ceremony continued. Still, Carol dutifully moved ahead with her program, apparently unaware of the disruption and afterward calling the assembly a great success. As far as I knew, she never said a word about the disruptions, never asked about the Exlax, during or after the event. It's as if she never noticed. But students did, and teachers did, and whether or not the laxative truly created digestive chaos or was just the centerpiece of well-crafted mischief remains a mystery.

My first period social studies class was a shoot-from-the-hip experiment. The only hint of some structure or curriculum came in the words of Mrs. Murray, our team's lead teacher, a big, manly woman with short-cropped gray hair.

"Go from the Civil War and try to get through World War II." That was the extent of her advice. No ideas for lesson plans, no direction. Being a very green rookie, I expected more. The only thing Mr. Cruz, my co-teacher for the period, and I had to work with was a set of textbooks—worn, torn, and beaten.

"And if I don't get to World War II?" I asked.

"Then you don't," Mrs. Murray said.

"Any particular historical period I should emphasize?"

"Hey, if you get them to understand who Abe Lincoln was, you're on to something."

There was nothing in my cohort program, my summer teaching, that could have prepared me for the shockingly directionless approach to teaching in District 131. I wasn't trained in any way to be a social studies teacher, but there I was trying anything that seemed reasonable, and in many ways making it up as I went along. I wasn't alone. There were plenty of teachers throughout East Aurora working from the seat of their pants, guessing, teaching simply what they *believed* should be taught.

"Don't be so worried about it all. You just do what you gotta do," said Mr. Cruz, who had been teaching at Cowherd for a couple of years. He called himself the "Puerto Rican," came from Chicago's southwest side, often talked about the rough neighborhood where he grew up, and prided himself on being the man from "the hood." He was certain he was the one who could truly relate to Cowherd's students. "It is what it is, man. Care about the kids and the rest will work itself out. Most of the administration doesn't know what they're talking about, anyway."

Stories surfaced frequently about teachers just doing whatever they wanted in classrooms. One teacher at East High was rumored to be teaching Satanism in one of the history classes, just because he could. There were complaints, eventually, and the administration caught up with him. But, like many other

David W. Berner

East High stories, it was hard to separate truth from fiction.

There was no satanic figure in the lesson plans of my social studies class. Instead, I had to deal with the American industrialists. We had made it through the Civil War, the carpetbaggers, Reconstruction, and it was time to look at wealth and industry in the U.S. The students were put into groups of two and three and each assigned an industrialist to research and then present their findings to the class. We spent days in the library, walking them through the process of gathering information for a project of this size, something most had never done. One group had the Rockefeller family. Diego was in that group.

"Rockefeller was gay."

These were the opening words of Diego's presentation, said so matter-of-factly, with such confidence, that I had to stifle a snicker. Mr. Cruz didn't bother. His laugh busted out from deep in his gut.

"Diego," Mr. Cruz questioned, sarcastically, but still laughing. "Rockefeller was gay?"

"Oh yeah, pipe smoker."

"Diego," I said, trying to stay disciplined and authoritative. "He wasn't gay. What else you got?"

"I think his whole family was gay."

The rest of the class, after initially being stunned by Diego's opening assertion, was now giggling.

"Was he really gay?" one student asked, looking at me for an answer.

"No, get off the gay thing," Mr. Cruz said, this time with a little more control.

Diego had done what he always loved to do, shock.

The Rockefeller incident helped me see that I was improving at facing, dealing with, all that a class could throw at me. Certainly this was no disaster, just a disruption. But frequently dealing with such things had built confidence, and I was beginning to understand how to accept these students for what they were, work with what they brought me. I was learning to stay calm, not to get rattled, and if I did, I found a way to get past it without losing focus, control.

Still, despite what Hollywood movie scripts about the teaching life might have implied, it was foolish to assume every day in class would be a revelation. My marriage may have benefited from understanding this. During the time I was trying to save my relationship with Marie through the weekly work with a therapist, I was expecting epiphanies. I was waiting for a light to shine on the answers to everything that was wrong. I failed to see that fixing what was broken wasn't going to happen through some great awakening, but it would come in the daily work, the awareness of what was needed in a marriage one day at a time.

After a couple days of presentations, it was time for Monopoly money. I wanted to give the students a chance to think and feel, and maneuver, like investors, to understand how a capitalist economy worked. Money and competition seemed a good way to accomplish this.

Students were given five thousand dollars each in play money to purchase and sell pretend-stock. They picked shares to buy out of the newspaper and followed them daily, learning the dynamics of why stock prices go up and down in real time, related to real events of the day.

"We can use the cash and buy anything we want, right?" asked one student on the morning of the lesson.

"Yep. Anything," I said.

Students scanned the listings and I helped decipher the symbols. Choosing a stock became a very personal matter, and somewhat stereotypical. The girls picked GAP Inc., Revlon, and SKECHERS USA, the footwear company. The boys chose Harley-Davidson Inc., Ford Motor Company, and World Wrestling Entertainment.

"Playboy! Oh yeah!" It was Diego, at it again. "It's in here. It really is. No shit."

"Yes, Playboy is a company. They have publishing, videos," I said.

"This is the same Playboy with the naked chicks, right?" said Diego.

"Same one."

75

"Cool, I'm buying five thousand dollars' worth, man."

I had come to expect Diego's outbursts, even accept them, but that wasn't true for everyone.

"Diego, shut the fuck up," said Elena as she combed her hair and checked her makeup in a compact mirror. She had given up on the stock search. "I'm so tired of your bullshit."

"Elena, that's enough," I said. "You and I need to talk. See me after class."

I hated saying those words. They had the typical tone of a disciplinarian, an old-fashioned schoolmaster.

Elena rolled her eyes as she had done so many times, flipped her hair, and pretended to ignore me. Then, she locked her eyes on me, cocked her head, and paused for a moment, appearing to get herself prepared for an important question.

"Are you trying to date my mother?"

"Elena, what are you talking about," I said.

"I think you're trying to go out with my mother."

"Come here," I said, waving my hand to get her to follow me into the hallway where the conversation could be more private. "Explain, please."

"You're always calling her. You phoned her several times last week. Left messages. I think you want to go out with my mother."

"Elena, I'm regularly calling your mother because of *you*. I call her to update her on your school work, your lack of motivation, your outbursts, and because you're failing every class you have with me," I said.

Elena's mother worked nights, leaving Elena home alone talking on the phone for hours. Sometimes she would sneak out, to—as her mother said—"be with the wrong people." Her mother suspected Elena was smoking dope, drinking. In class, Elena openly called herself "stupid" and would shut down during a lesson, saying she didn't understand, even if she did. It was easier to be "stupid."

"I'm sure your mother is a very nice woman, but Elena, this is about you, not your mother. Do you see that?" I said, giving her a moment to comprehend what I was trying to explain. She stared at me, her defiant expression slowly softening. "Elena, I'm not trying to date your mother."

She rolled her eyes and glanced at the floor.

"Yeah, whatever," she said.

"I don't want you to fail, Elena. Neither does your mother."

She walked back into the classroom with a bit of swagger, trying to prove to her classmates that whatever I said to her in the hallway had been immediately dismissed. Even if any of my words had made the slightest impact, she would never have allowed her friends to see that.

Elena quickly became, as many of the veteran teachers called it, my project child. I was determined to get her to believe in herself, get her to pass, and yes, I continued to telephone her mother.

Later that day, the Elena incident behind me, a little secret got out.

"Is it your birthday, Mr. Berner?" one student asked as I monitored the hallways just before lunch. "I heard it from some kid."

"It's my birthday, that's for sure," I said. One of the other teachers on the team must have let the secret slip out.

"How old?"

"I'm forty-seven."

"That means forty-seven punches, you know?" he said, smiling, making a fist, and waving it in front of me. This was the ritual usually reserved for dads, uncles, brothers, and friends.

"Yeah, forty-seven," another student said, making a second fist, and encouraging others to join in. Six boys came together, enthusiastically preparing to wallop their teacher.

"One, two, three, four…"

They were rhythmically singing out the numbers, simultaneously winding up and pounding my upper right arm to the beat of the numbers.

"Five, six, seven, eight…"

Mrs. Murray grimaced. Mr. Cruz nearly jumped in to break

it up. But I waved him off.

The forty-seventh punch was a real knockout, just as it's supposed to be. My arm pulsated with pleasant pain, the kind that makes you laugh, the kind boys share in the ritual of initiation.

The boys scooted down the hall to lunch, yelling out Happy Birthday wishes as I tried to rub out the sting they had left with me. As the hall emptied, Elena, all alone, stepped out from behind her locker door.

"Your birthday, huh?" she said.

"Yep, my b-day," I said.

"Well, Happy Birthday," she said, giving me a playful tap on the arm. "But you're pretty old."

She giggled, turned, and disappeared through the double doors and into the hallway to the cafeteria.

Chapter 9

On the backseat of my red 1991 Jeep Cherokee sat several cardboard boxes stuffed with dozens of books, not as many as I could have taken, but most. Until I started packing, I didn't realize how many of them were mine, but I would have felt like a thief leaving the shelves of what was now Marie's house nearly bare. It was a mixed collection—a 1961 volume set of Hemingway novels I found years ago in a used bookstore in a small town in central Illinois, journalism books including *Live from the Battlefield* by Peter Arnett—the former CNN reporter, books on the mechanics of the golf swing, and books on travel to Scotland and Ireland. I threw most of my clothes—still on the hangers—my guitar, and a stack of CDs into the Jeep's rear payload compartment. On the front seat was one of three antique typewriters I had collected over the years, including my favorite, a clunky black upright Royal from the 1920s. The Jeep was a rucksack on wheels, the carry-on baggage for the one-way journey to my new home. Not the exact place where Marie had driven me and asked me to remain close by, but the same neighborhood, the same three-bedroom style duplex just three blocks from the life I had known.

"David, I want you to take the piece your dad built. He made it for you," said Marie, walking through the house we had lived in together, surveying what would go with me and what would stay behind. My father was a carpenter by hobby, a craftsman who had created pieces of furniture with only hand tools. I had given him a sketch of a piece I wanted for my first apartment out of college. He created it to perfection—a pine, waist-high liquor cabinet with inlaid white tile on the counter.

"Thank you, Marie," I said, running my hand along the side and front of the lightly stained pine. "This means a lot."

The cabinet, a reclining blue leather chair, a bookcase with glass doors, and an expandable teak wood table that had once been the kitchen table in Marie's childhood home, a table I believed would make a wonderful desk, were hoisted into the flatbed of my brother-in-law's Dodge pickup truck. A bed, a clothes dresser, a brown leather couch and chair, a TV, and two standing lamps were being delivered from a furniture and electronic store—new purchases for a new life.

Marie, her brother, the boys, and my sister Diane—who had traveled from Pennsylvania—all agreed to help me move.

"Let's make it a family thing, an adventure," I told Marie, the day before the move. "Let's not make this an ending, let's make this a *beginning*."

We kept the experience lighthearted, drank a few beers as we lugged and carried, and ordered pizza to celebrate, to christen the new home.

"You said I can paint my room any color I want, right, Dad?" asked Graham, surveying the smallest of the home's three bedrooms, the room where he would sleep when he stayed with me.

"Yep, go for it," I said, hoping to give them some empowerment in this new family arrangement.

"Black. All black," said Graham.

"Hold on, buddy. Black?" I said, considering the three or four coats needed to make the walls truly colorless.

"Black. Absolutely. You said any color."

"Yeah, but black? You mean the walls, and everything?"

"Well, yeah." He seemed now to be questioning his first impulse. He looked around inside the square room, at the walls and the brownish carpet. "Okay. Maybe, ah, red?"

"Good, red it is."

The paint store labeled the color Fire Engine.

Casey chose orange for his room; Tequila Sunrise was the name on the can. Orange is not my favorite, but I meant what I said—any color, black notwithstanding.

That night the boys and their dog, Hogan, slept at my place. I bought futons for their rooms, but on this first night, we took the mattresses, blankets, and pillows to the living room floor. It was like camping out. We made popcorn, wrestled with the dog, and considered posters to put on the walls of their rooms—The Simpsons, Star Wars, Scooby-Doo.

"Guys, this is going to be all right. I'm just down the street, and you never have to ask to come over here. Just walk in the door. This is your house, too."

Our eyes were trained on the ceiling, our backs on the mattresses, the dog lying tight against my left leg, his head on Graham's belly.

"We can sleep here anytime, right, Dad?" Graham said, turning from his back to his side and snuggling against the blanket.

"As long as your mother's okay with it. You bet."

"And you're still coming for dinner on Sundays?" Casey asked, fighting to keep his sleepy eyes open.

"Always," I said. "It's our family time. Mom and I have decided."

The moonlight cast the sharp shadow of the backyard's twenty-foot maple tree through the curtain-less window and across our bodies. We were giving in, one by one—Hogan, then Graham and Casey—to what the day's work had done. I was the last to let go, not quite ready to allow the night to overtake me. Instead, I lay in the quiet darkness listening to the soft rhythm of the boys' sleepy breathing.

Hector was built like a Hummer—big-boned, bulky, ready

for battle. He probably weighed two hundred pounds and measured just an inch or two short of six foot. You could see his head above the other students in the crowded, claustrophobic Cowherd hallways. Size is about all that distinguished him, except for occasionally smuggling a hotrod magazine—*Motor Trend* was his favorite—into class to sneak a peek under his textbook. But when Hector got mad, he boiled over, and the violence that followed was proportionally far more intense than his reason for being upset in the first place.

It was between classes, and I was supposed to be standing guard outside my door, an administrative rule. Instead, I was putting student homework away at my desk. That's when I heard it—the unmistakable sound of bodies crashing against metal lockers.

"Fight, fight!"

Voices screamed from the hallway.

What made me run into the middle of it, I simply don't know. It was reactive, instinctual.

I pushed my way through the crowd and found Hector charging at another student, a considerably smaller one. Dozens of students cheered and chanted.

"Hit him!"

"Go, go!"

"Let's see blood!"

I jumped in front of Hector just as he lunged again at his target. His weight nearly knocked me to the ground. Grabbing the fabric of his shirt at the shoulders, I held on tight and forced my face into his.

"Hector, don't."

His cheeks were devil red; his fists clenched, emotions churned inside, his body quivered.

"Hector, no," I said, trying now to block him from twisting past me.

"I'll kill the fucker, I'll kill 'im!" he growled. Then he spun away from his nemesis and me, and slammed his fist into the lockers on the opposite side. Blood splattered from his knuckles.

"Ughhh!"

The punch was a pressure valve releasing pent-up rage. Hector sank against the lockers and slid down to the floor, his face expressionless.

Mr. Cruz marched the other student farther down the hallway, away from Hector and the action. The crowd of students quickly scattered, fearing the trouble they'd be in if they were caught in any part of this.

Hector was limp. He wouldn't look at me. I took him into my classroom, closed the door, and demanded to know what had triggered this.

"I just got mad," he said. "He just pissed me off."

It certainly was more than that, but Hector wouldn't reveal the details.

"I just want to go." He looked at me. "Can I go?"

He needed more time for cooling off. So, we stayed in the room for several minutes, both of us quiet. I allowed him to read his *Motor Trend.*

We never reported the fight. If we had, both boys would have been suspended. I didn't want that, and neither did Mr. Cruz. Sometimes there was nothing to gain from suspensions.

This wasn't the only fight at Cowherd; in fact, there were several. But this was my first.

"You did good, Mr. Berner," Mr. Cruz said, smiling. "You got right in the middle of it. Outstanding. Guess you're no longer a rookie."

Maybe not, but there were plenty of other rookie experiences to witness. Like the girls who self-mutilated, purposely cutting themselves until they bled and scarred. There were the random fires: one set in the boys' bathroom in the eighth grade hall, another near the gymnasium—both in trash cans. There was the apparent suicide attempt in the girls' eighth grade bathroom. Students said the girl cut up her wrists using a tool from one of the sewing classes. Very little blood, but still the rumors were flying—*she stabbed herself in the heart, she bled all over the floor, the bathroom tile turned red, she used a butcher knife.* The act wasn't as dramatic as it was troubling. She was treated at a hospital, saw counselors, and remained out of class for months. But the full details on what really happened, again, were hard to determine.

No matter how much I believed I had settled in at the school, figured the place out, thought I was ready for anything, the reality was—no one got used to what happened at Cowherd.

"Every year there's something," Mrs. Murray once told me. "Someone in somebody's family is shot, arrested. There's a student sent to juvenile court. The only thing you get used to is knowing there will be an unsettling event of some kind, probably several. I don't care how long you've been here. If you care, it makes you crazy."

And Mrs. Murray cared. You saw her routinely putting her arms around kids as she walked through the halls, talking to them in gentle tones. She loved being a teacher. But the years at Cowherd appeared to be wearing her down. She had health problems, was getting close to retirement age, and wondered aloud how long she could keep up this kind of work. She battled with the administration frequently over policies, curriculum, and discipline matters. She talked about how she had marched in the protests in the 1960s, and it was simply part of her nature to stand up for what she believed, question and fight authority. She was vocal, sincere, and unflinching, and the students knew she was on their side, even when she was tough with them.

Friday night was beer night. Several teachers, at precisely 3:15, minutes after the last student was gone, headed for The Fox and Hound, a bar just a few miles from Cowherd. Carly was the self-appointed coordinator.

"You going tonight?" she asked, tipping an imaginary glass to her lips.

Carly had been stopping by my classroom during my preparation period a couple of times a week to say hello, and making sure I was in on the end-of-the-week celebration. On this Friday, the day of the fight, a beer sounded like some very good medicine.

"Yeah, I need it today," I said. "Give me just a couple of minutes to enter these grades."

"Oh, come on, Berner, for Christ's sake. Give it up. You better be right behind me. No excuses."

"I'll be there, promise."

I liked that Carly came around. Not only was she stunning to look at, but it was flattering to have a pretty young lady encouraging me to join her for a drink. Who wouldn't want that?

The only people in the tavern in the mid-afternoon on a Friday were teachers who punched out earlier than workers in the nine-to-five world. Five of us, including Carly and Bill, one of the teachers who had taught me how to take matters into my own hands when it came to what I needed out of the supply closet, took a table near the bar.

"First rule. No talking about work," Carly announced. "No exceptions."

"Oh, come on, we have to have something to complain about," said Bill, lifting a bottled beer to his mouth.

"Nope. And if you want to complain, we'll help you find something else to rip on."

"No problem there. I can talk about my ex-wife," Bill said, shaking his head and knocking back another swig.

Bill's situation could simply be described as a mess. He had spent months, if not years, in court, fighting his ex-wife, trying to gain full custody of his children. Very few of us knew the whole story.

"I may know something in a few days. Lawyer thinks we might be getting close."

"Crazy bitch," said Carly. "It'll work out, Bill. It has to." Then, holding a mug of draft in her hand, Carly turned to me. "And what about you? What's your deal?"

"Me? No deal. My wife and I, *former* wife, get along. We work hard at it," I said. "Lucky, I guess."

Carly's eyes stayed fixed on me, as if she were waiting for me to reveal something more, something juicy. She took another swallow of beer.

"But you're divorced, right?" she asked, confirming what

she already knew.

"Yeah," I said, still not comfortable admitting my marriage had failed.

"So then, why are you still wearing the ring?"

The simple gold wedding band remained on the third finger of my left hand. I had considered removing it on the day Marie and I were officially, legally divorced. It's what you're supposed to do, I figured. But I couldn't. I wasn't ready. I still wasn't.

With the thumb of my left hand, I twisted the ring around on my finger.

"I don't know. I guess I haven't thought about it."

"Well, you're thinking about it now, right? So let's take it off," said Carly.

"Now?"

"Why not? I can even help you."

Carly put down her beer, grabbed my left wrist with one hand, and wrapped the fingers of the other around the gold band, her red-painted nails reflecting the light from the bar lamps.

"No, no, that's okay," I said, attempting to pull away from her grip. "I don't think you can get it off anyhow. Not without some soap or water or something."

"Maybe a little beer?"

Carly dipped her fingers in my half-full mug as if she were soaking her cuticles, then rubbed the brew over the ring.

"This ought to help it," she said, laughing and wiggling the band back and forth just below the knuckle.

"You're not ready," she said, quickly taking her hands away from mine as if she had mistakenly touched a hot stove-top skillet. "But you will be. It's coming."

We ordered another round as the talk turned to pets, music, books, and a vow to try a new bar next Friday. But I was less attentive to the conversation, and instead searched the hands of nearby customers for the rings they wore, the wedding bands that linked them to the people they loved, thought they did, once did. Using the index finger and thumb of my right hand, I gently rotated my own ring around the finger it encircled, rubbing away a smudge, a blemish on the gold.

"Give me your cell number," Carly said, punching the keys on her mobile. "I'm putting you in my contacts, Berner. I'm calling you when we caravan to that new place next week. I want to make sure you don't get lost."

There was one swallow left at the bottom of my second beer mug. I lifted it, letting the now room temperature brew hit the back of my throat, and placed the thick, heavy glass on the table.

I gave Carly the number.

"And I don't plan to get lost," I said. "Wouldn't think of it."

Chapter 10

The cramps were awful, bad enough to make me wince and double over. The pain would sneak up on me, turn sharp, and maintain its intensity for over a minute; then it would happen again. By the third time I knew I had to find a way out of my classroom and into the bathroom. But you just can't leave a room full of eighth grade students with no one in charge.

It was either that or crap my pants.

"Guys, while you're working on what's on the board, well, I'll be right back," I said, hustling through the door and down the hall to the boys' bathroom, squeezing my butt cheeks together as I moved.

The bathroom was empty. I sat inside one of the door-less stalls—door-less, I was told, because students had been known to shut the doors and do drug deals as they stood on the toilet seats. I don't know what made me sick, but I obviously had something—a bug, the twenty-four-hour virus. I moved as quickly as possible to clean myself up and get back to the classroom, praying that things weren't in chaos.

When you teach in the public school system you're trapped in a classroom. And you're told never to abandon it for any reason. Those students are your responsibility. Their safety is your job. If something happens—a fight, a fire, anything—and you aren't there to handle it, you can be reprimanded, even fired. It is that simple.

As I moved toward the classroom door, I could hear the voices of the students, but oddly, surprisingly, nothing rowdy or loud. I walked in slowly, almost tiptoeing, as if a more dramatic entrance would upset the balance of things.

Nearly everyone was in a seat, some concentrating on the assigned project, a few others talking casually, calmly with other students. I was stunned. I wanted to double-check the room number. Was this the same group of students who had started the school year with me?

"Everything going good, guys?" I asked, tentatively, softly, almost as if saying anything louder would spark frenetic disruption.

The few students who were standing began to find their seats. Those who were talking with friends ended their conversations and began to focus on the project, the work left on the blackboard.

"Can you explain what the second item on the board is, mister? I don't get it," one student asked.

It was nearly Christmas break. I had been at Cowherd for over four months, but only now was I aware of the changes, the evolution that had taken place. In that time, I had somehow created—through hard work, luck, and happenstance—a manageable, workable classroom. The evidence was now right in front of me.

Despite my sour stomach and ravaged gastro-intestinal system, I felt pretty darn good about things.

I didn't want to leave school early that day. I had plans to talk to Carly after the students left, a question to ask. But with my bad stomach, I decided it would be better to wait, and head home for now.

My bed was a dream to climb into. I had the leftovers of Sunday's *New York Times* to work through, and resting with the newspaper was good medicine. And it was, but the phone conversation I had received earlier in the week was on my mind. The call came from the chair of the Radio Department at Columbia College Chicago.

"Why would you want this position?" she asked.

"I always wanted to teach college. Plus, I had taught off and on for years at that level as adjunct faculty."

She asked about my education, my broadcast industry experience, if I would take some time to look at the class descriptions in the department's catalog, and if I would consider another discussion in a couple of days. I had hoped to someday, eventually, teach college, but I didn't expect Cowherd to get in the way.

A colleague from my early Chicago radio days, now working at Columbia, had phoned me sometime around Thanksgiving and asked if I would be interested in a full-time, tenure-track faculty position opening up at Columbia College in the city. She had been at the school some ten years after leaving the radio station where we both had worked. At first, I was excited. This was what I wanted, right? Then, apprehension slowly enveloped me. Not necessarily about *taking* a new job, but about *leaving* the one I had. Could I walk out Cowherd's door? Leave the students? Could I walk away from what they were giving me? These teenagers had helped me begin to reinvent myself, put some passion back in my life, and it only became apparent when there was another option available, only when there was a real chance I would say good-bye to Cowherd.

My failed marriage had been a similar journey. I didn't see what I needed to see, to feel, to discover until the realization of a divorce was right in front of me. Then, there was my father's health. Not until the cancer began eating away at him, and there was the real chance of losing him, did I comprehend how much impact my father had on my life. I thought about Marie, the boys, who I was, who I had become. I had found a new place that was fueling a new passion—why would I want to say good-bye?

I eventually fell asleep with two pillows propped behind my head and the remnants of the *Times* scattered on my lap and the floor at the side of the bed.

When I was an undergrad, my girlfriend and I hopped inside a buddy's rusted, run-down Pontiac. I think it was a Pontiac, but I couldn't be sure. It had four wheels and it started. That's all that mattered in those days. With my friend and his girl in the front seats, we took a road trip to Kent State University. We wanted to see where the students were shot.

It was about a three-hour drive from our school in the middle of Pennsylvania to the Ohio school that had become infamous for violence in the days when demonstrations against the Vietnam War were rising up on campuses across the country. On May 4, 1970, Ohio National Guard troops fired into groups of students. Four were killed, nine wounded. Students at dozens of other colleges, even middle schools, throughout America held student strikes. Just five days after the shootings, 10,000 people demonstrated in Washington DC against the war and the killing of the four at Kent. These were the days of Richard Nixon, burning draft cards, and Woodstock.

For whatever reason, the trip we took in 1977 was heavy on my mind the morning I awoke from my twelve-hour, illness-induced sleep. My stomach was greatly improved and my head clear again. But why Kent State?

The shootings had been an obsession with my friends and me. The vinyl version of the Crosby, Stills, Nash and Young song, "Ohio," was frequently on one of our turntables. I played the song on my guitar. And we talked often about the facts and details of those days at Kent State, the news reports that were now more than seven years old.

"That could have been one of us," said Tracey, my girlfriend, as we traveled down Interstate 80 across the Pennsylvania-Ohio border. "That could be me lying on the ground, dead."

We had a crude map of the campus pulled from the pages of an encyclopedia, and we drove around the school, trying to be inconspicuous, searching for the spot where the shootings took place. After getting lost and becoming frustrated, we pulled the car over and asked a student.

"We can't just say, *Hey, man, where'd the students get shot?*" Tracey said.

That did seem a bit insensitive.

"I heard there was a plan to build a new gymnasium or library or something on or near the site," I said. "And there's a lot of controversy over it. So, why don't we just ask where the new building might go up?"

That seemed a simple solution.

"Excuse me," I said, as we turned the car in a parking lot, and rolled down a window before a student carrying several books, apparently on his way to or from class. "Can you tell us where the school is thinking about constructing that new building?"

"Oh, you want to see where the students were shot?"

Apparently, we weren't the only hippies making a trip to Kent State.

That memory stayed with me much of the early morning and my drive to Cowherd. At the time, it seemed an odd part of the past to inexplicably arise out of the deep sections of my memory. But when I think about it now, it makes more sense. I was juggling deep thoughts during my days at Cowherd, consciously and unconsciously, about who I was, where I had been, what I wanted to be, what I was passionate about, what had shaped me. Maybe it wasn't so unusual for the memory of a road trip, one I had been compelled to take, to surface so keenly at a time when I was redefining my life.

Inside my mailbox in the main office that morning was a nondescript yellow sheet of paper, a substitute assignment. The papers would show up when we were expected to replace an absent teacher during our scheduled prep time. Cowherd had a system that discouraged the administration from hiring a lot of substitutes and expanding the budget. Instead, full-time teachers already at the school would fill the holes. It was cheaper.

My assignment was seventh period girls' phys ed.

I didn't mind subbing, but it had become a semi-regular duty, at least three times a week, and it took time away from preparing for my own classes. Teachers at Cowherd routinely called in sick when they weren't. They were nearly as bad as the students.

I had subbed sixth grade language arts, a sewing class, a seventh grade math class, and even a music class. But gym was new, and it was far different than anything I had done before.

Gym classes were combined—girls and boys—with at least three teachers assigned to a swarm of students, half of whom didn't even bother to properly dress, wearing their jeans and T-shirts instead of the assigned phys-ed shorts and shirt. Every sound echoed and reverberated off the concrete walls and wooden floor of the gymnasium, making the voices of the teachers impossible to understand. Only the blowing of a neck whistle would turn the heads of the students. The boys and girls were separated only by space, and each student had an assigned spot to sit for attendance. The teachers took an exorbitant amount of time, wasting about a quarter of the class period, just to mark absences.

I watched as the other teachers attempted to herd students into place, a task that seemed pointless, hopeless. Most of the students had no interest in being there, paid little attention to the teachers. Instead, they ran around playing tag or shooting basketballs into one of the four hoops. And the teachers didn't seem to care, marking anyone absent who wasn't in their assigned spot.

I wasn't sure what I was supposed to be doing. The lone female teacher handled attendance for me and barely acknowledged my presence.

"They're supposed to play basketball today," she said, giving an order and handing me the completed attendance book for the students. "Just let them shoot hoops."

That was it. *Just let them shoot hoops.* I guess I had anticipated something more. Apparently, just keeping them busy was the only goal.

"Hey, Mr. Berner, you our sub?"

Those words came from behind me somewhere. I turned and saw Suzana, a student from one of my language arts class, a good kid with decent manners, one of the few, and smarts that barely had been acknowledged or recognized by any of the teachers.

"Yep, Suzana, it's me. You got me."

"Bet I can shoot more free throws than you," she said, tossing a basketball from one hand to the other, smiling slyly as if she had a secret to keep.

"You giving me a challenge?"

Suzana was on the eighth grade girls' basketball team. She was rather tall and big for her age, big-boned, you might say. Actually, she was a little overweight. But she was reasonably athletic, and that was about all you needed to make the team.

"Oh, I can beat you, I know it," she said. "Ms. Rousseau's been working with me."

Ms. Rousseau was Nora, from my graduate cohort. She had been assigned as a seventh grade science teacher at Cowherd and had agreed to coach the eighth grade girls' basketball team when no one else stepped forward. Nora handled the school administration like she did her fellow cohort members—with an edgy, matter-of-fact, ultra-honest approach. It didn't always work for her. Nora didn't compromise well, didn't like authority much, and clashed with the old guard at Cowherd. But the students on the team loved her. She treated them with respect, challenged them, and made them into competitors.

"Suzana, you're on," I said.

Standing just a few feet from us was another familiar face. Lucia, my tough girl, had been listening to Suzana and me talk. Lucia had one hand on her waist and dribbled a basketball with the other.

"What are you doing here?" she asked, sneering.

"Subbing. You in this class?"

"Ah, yeah, of course," she said, rolling her eyes, wondering if I could possibly ask a more ridiculous question.

"Suzana says she can take me on free throws."

"Oh, she can take you, all right."

"You in on this?" I asked.

"You think you can beat *me*? You *serious*?"

Suzana was tossing a few balls through the nearby hoop but could hear the exchange with Lucia.

"Come on, Mr. Berner," Suzana said. "You want some warm-ups?"

I acknowledged her question, but responded directly to Lucia.

"All three of us," I said. "We'll count the free throws. The one with the most wins."

Lucia said nothing and methodically dribbled the ball over to the free throw line. She took a shot. It banked off the backboard and went in. She twisted quickly on the hardwood floor, her athletic shoes squeaking, and looked directly at me, a stare of superiority.

"Let's get this thing started," I said, pumping out my chest and having a little fun with the moment. I never was a good basketball player. In fact, in high school pick-up games I was chosen somewhere in the middle. Despite this, I figured I could handle a few free throws with eighth grade girls. I could make it close, at least.

Suzana took the first shot. Nothing but net. She passed to Lucia. Another shwoosh. I banked mine and made it. Suzana again, and again a shwoosh. Lucia spun one around the rim. Straight in. I missed my next two, miserably. Suzana smiled. Lucia said nothing, her game face on. Suzana then made six in a row. Lucia made five. At the end of the period, when the girls were called to head for the lockers, Suzana had fourteen baskets, Lucia twelve. I had six.

"Mr. Berner, you're pretty good," Suzana said. "Just rusty, huh?"

Lucia ignored the instructions to stop and head for the lockers, continuing to dribble and shoot layups, pacing the shots just enough to ask a question.

"When was the last time before this that you shot basketball?"

"Summertime," I said.

"Yeah, figures."

"Why you say that?"

She continued to dribble, shoot, and talk.

"You need work. First, you should jump *into* the shot. You jump falling back. That sucks."

Lucia stopped and held the ball against her waist with the inside part of her left forearm.

"You ought to come to one of our games and watch how to do it. Watch us play." She dribbled again and turned to set up for a long shot. "But you probably won't."

"When's the next home game?" I said.

Lucia tossed the ball toward the basket, watching it rim out and hit the floor.

"You're not coming," she said, almost demanding that I wouldn't. "Nobody comes." She took another shot. "No big deal."

Suzana and nearly every other student had gone inside the locker room, leaving Lucia alone with me on the far side of the gym. I retrieved the ball after it banked off the backboard from Lucia's last shot and held it in my hand.

"You gotta go," I said, nodding toward the locker room door.

Lucia took her time walking away, her back to me. At that moment, the tough girl didn't look so tough. I watched her disappear through the double door into the locker room. Standing solitary in the gym, I dribbled the ball a few times and took a shot. It hit the square on the backboard and fell in, flipping the net as the ball dove through it, and creating echoes in the cavernous, empty gymnasium as the rubber ball hit hardwood.

On my drive home from Cowherd that night, the chair of the Radio Department at Columbia College phoned and asked if I would formally apply for the available teaching position at the university, and if I would be willing to teach one class before a panel that would observe my educational style and abilities. I immediately, almost instinctively, agreed. Then, after I hung up my cell phone, I began to sweat. I felt hollow, empty, unsettled. I turned my car into a strip mall parking lot and sat in the driver's seat, staring at the passing traffic. Big decisions would have to be made, and I was far from prepared to make them. Better to think about the here and now, I thought.

I searched my briefcase for Cowherd's basketball schedule. I had a game to attend.

Chapter 11

It was a Monday, early evening. I parked my car in the far lot on the west side of the university and walked to my cohort's night class. My cell phone rang.

"Dave? It's your sister. Dad was at the doctor today and I just wanted to update you."

The staccato delivery of her words was different than all the other updates.

"It's not very good, Dave."

"Tell me what they said," I asked, afraid of what I might hear.

"The doctor is not sure why nothing is slowing the cancer. They're not saying it exactly, but they're giving up, Dave. You can tell they're just trying to manage it now. And, Dave, he's lost more weight. He hurts, he just hurts."

"How's his spirits?"

"Bad, just bad."

We both had known this was coming, but neither of us would admit it out loud.

"How's Mom?" I asked.

"She's okay. She's strong, Dave."

"How are you?"

I was terribly worried about her. She had been watching my father deteriorate from close range.

"I'm all right, I guess."

"Do you need me to come home?"

"No. No, not yet. I promise I'll tell you when it's time."

"Can I talk to him?"

"He's sleeping right now. Call him later. But be ready, he's not good."

There wasn't anything anyone could do for Dad.

My sister being near him was good, not only for Dad, but for me, too. She had taken a leave of absence from her job as a produce worker at the local supermarket chain to help my mother care for him. And although I telephoned nearly every day, thought about him, prayed for him every day, I struggled with being five hundred miles away. I worried about my students, about basketball games, my graduate work, my children, whether Carly could be interested in me, and far away, inside the house where I grew up, my father was dying. What kind of a son is that?

I leaned against the outside wall of the student union building, put my hand over my eyes, and started to cry.

The latest rumor at Cowherd was about sex. A seventh grade boy and an eighth grade girl apparently got caught having intercourse in the storage area of Cowherd's gymnasium. The story was that they skipped class, in the middle of the day, and snuck into the area where the school stored the floor mats for wrestling. I'm sure you get the picture. One of our school deans couldn't help describe the discovery to some of the teachers.

"They were half undressed, tangled up together, panting. It was pathetic," he said.

Whether it was true or not didn't matter. The story spread quickly throughout the school, and nothing seemed to cool down this couple's relationship. Every day, the two clung to each other as they walked out of the school together—his hand tucked inside her right, rear jean pocket and her arm wrapped tightly around his neck.

It wasn't unusual to find students necking in the halls, tongues deep in throats, legs wrapped around each other. I broke up a few encounters. The first time is awkward, but then you learn—just barge right in and verbally hose them down. Hormones are hard to suppress. The boys talked about sex in the halls, usually boasting about encounters they could only wish for. And the girls, although they weren't supposed to, got away with wearing deep necklines, even semi-see-through material, albeit in the mandatory white or blue. Girls were frequently called to the office, usually by third period or so, and handed a standard white T-shirt from a stash of them in the administrative offices. The girls would pull the shirt over their revealing tops, but by then, it was too late. They had made their impression.

After-school events were another matter.

"They dress like hootchie-kootchie mamas," Mrs. Murray would say.

The girls had a pattern—go home after classes, ditch the mandatory school dress, and return to strut their stuff wearing tighter jeans, shorter shorts, tight tube-tops, and layers of makeup. And because it was *after* school, many got away with it.

The girls on the eighth grade basketball team knew not to push the limits of the dress code. If they did, the coach benched them. It was that simple. Every one of them remained within the rules during and after school. And on the day I stayed to watch an afternoon home game, keeping my earlier promise, all the girls were eligible to play. They had honored the dress code and kept their grades in reasonable shape, requirements to be in the lineup.

A loud call reverberated around the hardwood floor and the old wooden, rollout bleachers.

"Mr. Berner!"

Suzana spotted me making my way into the stands as the Cowherd team warmed up. A couple of other team members looked up, including Coach Rousseau, who smiled and waved back. Lucia saw me, too, and simply nodded her head in my direction the way acquaintances might quietly, unemotionally acknowledge each other.

I sat alone, leaned my elbows on the bench behind me, and settled in for the battle against Cowherd's rival, Simmons Middle School.

The crowd in the stands was sparse—a few parents, couple of teachers, a scattering of students. And for the first time, I saw the reality of the school's racial divide, a physical separation that had, for some reason, escaped me. Most of Cowherd's students were Hispanic, mainly of Mexican descent, but there were some twenty-five African-American students, maybe a couple dozen in eighth grade. In the stands, near the middle top row, four black boys sat together, two black girls sat three rows below them, and a small gathering of Hispanic students, maybe a dozen, sat and stood on the adjoining set of bleachers, near the bottom, easily thirty feet away. The divide never seemed this obvious in the classroom. But the sight of the split in the stands, for a moment, made me wonder about a silent schism, a tension that was rarely talked about, acknowledged. Other schools in the district had their share of racial confrontations, even physical fights, between students, and there was the story making the rounds of one African-American mother at the high school who had accused a Hispanic teacher of racism. The argument between the family, the teacher, and eventually the administration got pretty ugly. But at Cowherd, the issue of race had remained below the surface, and rarely addressed. Among the African-American boys in the stands was Adrian, an eighth grader in my first period social studies class. He was a pensive kid who showed flashes of being bright, aware, and curious. But like many of the academically sharper students in this district, it seemed to me that his smarts had not been nourished or cultivated through his school years. There was no reason for Adrian to stand out in the classroom. He never caused trouble, kept to himself much of the time, and like most of the other students, didn't do his homework, keeping him very much in the mainstream. It was the student who *completed* the homework that made the impression. But here, in the gymnasium bleachers, it was different. In this setting, Adrian was the center of attention, the leader, the boss of the boys in his group.

"What you think about that shot, Adrian?"

"Adrian, you goin' to Maria's party?"

"Adrian, you gonna play ball with the boys tomorrow?"

His friends wanted Adrian's attention; they wanted to be near him, liked by him, part of his world. And the girls? They loved him. Adrian was a handsome kid, with soft brown eyes and a strong jaw. He was pensive, in a mysterious, movie star sort of way. And in the gymnasium, the girls—the blacks and the Hispanics—stole glances at Adrian, giggled, and glanced again. He rarely glanced back.

Adrian and his friends paid far more attention to the girls on the court who were going through their pre-game routines. The boys talked about abilities, strategies, and who took better shots than others. Adrian was the most talkative; unusual for the Adrian I was familiar with. His quietness in class gave the impression he was unhappy, reclusive. It was good to see him enjoying himself. At one moment, he caught sight of me, but pretended he hadn't. Not cool to say hello to a teacher, and certainly not cool to do it after school hours.

The Cowherd team showed some spark and aggressiveness at the start and took an early lead. But by halftime the score was close, and in the third period Simmons came out with gusto and took control. In the final quarter, Cowherd rallied again, but Simmons hung on to its tenuous lead to win by four points.

The next morning, Lucia and Suzana stopped me in the eighth grade hallway before first period.

"We saw you there, Mr. Berner," Suzana said, slapping me on the back. "Too bad we couldn't win it."

"They cheated, ya know," Lucia said.

"They did, huh?" I asked.

"You see all those freakin' fouls? Come on, man, it was completely bogus. Fourth quarter? Ridiculous. You saw it. You had to see it?"

I wasn't about to argue with Lucia; I might have lost what I was gaining.

"Yeah, it was a bit iffy," I said.

"Freakin' bogus, man."

"Yeah, Lucia, sure looked bogus."

Suzana nodded her head, agreeing with Lucia. Suzana was too polite to openly make accusations. But Lucia? She was not afraid to accuse anyone of anything if she believed it to be true.

"Damn straight, Mr. Berner. Freakin' straight," Lucia said, strutting down the hall, watching Suzana hurry to class.

It was Friday and I was ready to make my move.

The week had gone well. I was falling into a comfortable, confident routine at Cowherd, my university work was under control, the boys were doing well, and Dad's condition, albeit bad, had remained stable since my sister's call earlier in the week. So, it was time. I was divorced, I was a good guy, and Carly obviously liked me. She even flirted with me, right?

I was at my desk alone during prep time when Carly stood at the door. She was simply stunning that day with her chestnut hair long to her shoulders, blue eye shadow around brown eyes, and a subtle red on her thin lips.

"I really could use a beer tonight," she said.

"I'm shocked." I laughed. "You, wanting a beer? I'm absolutely shocked."

Carly was easily ten years younger than me and still very much into having a few too many. I, on the other hand, was a one-beer kind of guy and always had been. At times, during the few months I had known Carly, I felt like her favorite uncle, not a potential date. But there were just as many other times when I was convinced sparks were flying. Earlier that day, I saw Carly in the hallway near the office and asked if she had a moment before the end of the day to stop by my classroom. "I want to ask you something," I said. It sounded so, well, high school. At least I didn't ask one of the other teachers to pass her a note.

"Everything cool?" Carly asked.

"Yeah, good week, no serious problems."

"Hey, didn't you want to talk to me about something?"

I'm sure there were beads of sweat forming on my forehead, and if nerve endings were visible you would have seen mine wiggling and squirming all over my body.

Carly adjusted her grip on the books and student papers she had in her hand and rested them against her hip. Her other hand ran through the bangs of her hair, brushing them straight back off her face, entwining her fingers in the silky strands.

Isn't it true, when women play with their hair, it's a sign that they are interested in you? I think I read that somewhere in *Esquire*.

"What are you doing, ah, a week from, ah, Friday?"

"Oh, that's my birthday, ya know? I think my boyfriend's got something planned. Why? What's going on?"

Shit. A *boyfriend*? How did that happen? How did I miss that? I had spent nearly a dozen evenings with Carly at our Friday night teacher get-togethers talking about everything, everything except the *boyfriend*. I suddenly felt creepy, like an old man stalking an underage girl.

"Oh," I said, turning my eyes away from her, pretending to straighten out the papers on my desk. "I was thinking about going to this club in the city where this folk artist plays. And, I was thinking about someone who might like that sort of music and, well, I was thinking of you."

"Cool. That would be great, but it's my birthday and all, and I'm sure plans are being made," she said with a little dance. Birthdays still meant a lot to her.

"Sure, yeah, I just thought, well, I understand, sure."

"Hey, thanks. Sounds like a nice time. Maybe if it weren't my birthday. But my birthday is party time. Got to party," she said, again doing that little dance.

Carly had no idea that she was being asked out on a date. It never even occurred to her. I was her pal, a friend, and that was that.

At the end of the day, I sat inside my car in the school parking lot, windows rolled up, not wanting to move. I left just minutes after students were dismissed, as early as I could, deciding not to meet Carly and the others for a beer. Not this night.

Chapter 12

Elena marched into sixth period. Clearly, she had something on her mind.

"Mr. Berner," she demanded, "I need to talk to you."

I pulled her aside away from the classroom door and the flow of students making their way to the desks. She took her stance, crossed her arms on her chest, her jaw clenched; her head shook sharply left and right in tight, quick movements.

"You have to stop calling my mother," Elena said, locking her eyes on mine.

"Elena," I said, talking softly and hoping to calm her down, "I think I *need* to keep talking to her."

"You're still trying to date my mother, aren't you?" Elena insisted on an immediate answer.

"We've been through this, Elena. I'm sure your mother is a nice lady, but I'm not trying to date her. When we talk, we talk about *you*."

She stood reticent, her arms still tightly crossed, her eyes now looking past me, as if wanting to dismiss what I said.

"Elena." I smiled. "Remember, I'm calling her because of *you*."

Elena shifted her weight back and forth, staring at her feet, the floor, to hide her eyes from mine. She stroked her black hair as if trying to soothe herself. I had been over this several times with Elena. She knew the real reason I was calling her mother, but had relentlessly asked if I had a romantic interest.

"Elena," I said, attempting to get her to look at me. "Are you all right?"

She kept her eyes to the ground, placed her hands on her hips, shifted her weight again, and took a single deep inward breath, blowing the air out in one sustained burst. Then, with her head still angled toward the floor, her eyes lifted up to meet mine.

"Don't you like my mother?"

With that single question, it was all finally clear. How could I have missed it? I felt ashamed for being so unaware, out of touch with what Elena was feeling.

I reached out and put my arm around her shoulder.

"Elena," I said, "please know this. Your mother is a very nice person. She cares about you. And, honestly, she will find someone, someday, a true companion. But right now, Elena, you are the biggest part of her life."

"Do you think she's pretty?" she asked.

"Elena, please understand. I call your mother to talk about *you*. You are our priority. That's all we talk about." I watched her eyes, darting up and down, refusing to look directly at me. "And next week, your mother is coming in."

"What?" she said panicked, her demeanor changing in an instant.

"She needs to come in so we can talk all together. It's important. It's not to scold you. It's to help you."

Elena abruptly brushed her hair away from her face, leaned against the hallway wall, and took another of those deep breaths.

"Yeah, whatever," she said, annoyed at the way the conversation was going. "I guess I get it."

"I hope so, Elena. I really do."

"What we gonna talk about?"

107

"I know you want to go to the high school," I said. "You won't, you know. Your friends will go and you'll stay behind if you don't get it together."

"Yeah, yeah, I get it."

"Having your mother come in and talk about what we can do as a group effort might be really helpful."

"Am I gonna flunk eighth grade?"

"Honestly, Elena, you could. But I'm here, your mother's here, and we're trying to keep that from happening. But you, *you* have to be willing to work harder."

"Yeah, yeah," she said, seemingly accepting a bit of the blame.

"Can you do that?"

Elena, like so many of Cowherd's students, didn't get much individual attention from teachers. Not to say some teachers didn't try. But, a phone call to a student's mother was unusual. I didn't see it that way. Maybe it was rookie exuberance. Maybe a lot of teachers once did what I did, but lost their enthusiasm when their efforts fell miserably short.

"Can I go back to my seat now?"

"Sure," I said. "You okay?"

"Yeah, I'm okay."

It was clear to me. Elena's need to have someone love and care for her mother, and more importantly, the need for a father figure in her young life had been weighing more heavily on her than anyone could have known. She was missing something, and I was the convenient solution. But it could have been any man, anyone showing any interest at all.

Earlier that day, just before the first period, Diego rushed into school squirting an aerosol can of whipped cream into his mouth. He zipped up and down the hallways sending blasts of the treat between the lips of others, student after student, each opening wide and demanding a taste.

"Diego, over here!"

"Hey, me, me!"

Diego spun his way around the eighth grade wing, spraying

the white foamy topping on begging tongues, sometimes missing and wasting globs of the cream on cheeks and noses.

"He's done that before," said Mrs. Murray. "It's breakfast."

It wouldn't have surprised anyone to learn that it was the only thing left in the refrigerator that morning at Diego's house. The tumultuous home life of our students, I was told, sometimes meant no food until the unemployment check came in the mail, or someone bothered to go to the grocery store.

Strangely enough, Diego's whipped cream breakfast was just the appetizer for a memorable lunch.

Spaghetti was on the menu that day, a big favorite. But pasta covered in marinara sauce is not the kind of food you want readily available when tempers flare.

One harsh word and the flick of a strand of pasta turned the lunchroom on its head. One student called another student's mother a "whore," triggering an immediate retaliation—a piece of pasta flew through the air, landing on the accusing kid's forehead. Then, in an instant, it was like that familiar, clichéd scene from the movie *Animal House*—an all-out food fight. Red sauce and pasta were splattered on the walls, the tables, the chairs, the fronts and backs of student shirts and pants, the floor, even the light fixtures. Teachers monitoring the lunch period said at least a dozen students jumped into the fray. In the big picture, it seemed a rather minor incident, albeit a messy one. But it took the veil off a deeper issue.

Later that afternoon, an undercurrent of tension made its way around the school—Hispanics and blacks, maybe as many as twenty-five kids, planned a fight, a big one, across the street from the school near the convenience store and gas station. First, there were rumblings in the halls from the students. Then, one of Cowherd's deans told some of the teachers what he had heard.

"This is not an idle threat," he said. "Apparently during the food fight some things were said between some black and Mexican students. We have some very pissed off kids."

During the last period of the day, Jim, the assistant principal, came to my classroom and called me into the hall.

"Keep an eye on your kids and an ear to what some of them are saying. Keep an eye on where they go after class. I think something is definitely up," he said.

Jim was no neophyte when it came to school violence. He had worked at a number of tough schools, and I heard he once was shot at during gang violence in one inner-city district. Not sure that it was true, but it certainly added to his legend. Jim looked the part of a no-nonsense administrator—a big, burly guy, with a voice to match, a former hockey player whose hair and beard had turned white with age. He looked like a mix between Santa Claus and a member of the World Wrestling Federation.

If the fight went down on school property there could be suspensions and expulsions. If it happened just off school grounds, police could take students into custody. East Aurora's police had been alerted. But Jim appeared ready to take matters into his own hands.

"I heard it's going to happen at the west corner. I'll be there, standing there, at the end of the day. Going to have some of the deans with me, too. We'll have the walkie-talkies so we can monitor what's going on in the school before they reach the corner," Jim said.

Jim was in his element, almost reveling in the possibility he could thwart this fight, diffuse any violence before it happened.

"These guys have threatened this before," Jim said, giving me a handwritten list of names of students he thought were involved. "But, I'll tell you, it's not going to happen under my watch."

When the last class was dismissed, I stood at my classroom door and watched for the targeted students. Everything appeared normal—students talking at lockers, the usual methodical exodus toward the doors. Then, at the far end of the hall, a group of five Hispanic boys began pushing their way through the crowd, marching as one toward the exit door. Heads turned as others watched them pass, momentarily assessing their purpose. Then, one by one, students fell in behind them and followed toward the door.

"There's going to be a fight," I heard one say.

"Niggers ain't gonna be alive," one growled.

"Fuck, yeah," another answered. "They're gonna get fucked up!"

I moved down the hall in the opposite direction searching for the dean. I wanted to be sure he saw what I saw. He was already on the walkie-talkie communicating with Jim.

"They're coming out the north door of the eighth grade wing."

"Got them," Jim's voice crackled through the small speaker.

The volume of voices in the hallway had ratcheted up, and you could feel a wave of hateful energy permeate the eighth grade wing like electricity moving through water.

"Race fight!"

"Whooh! Kick ass!"

"Motherfuckers ain't gonna get home."

Elena rushed past me behind the mob moving toward the exit.

"Elena. Stay out of it!" I yelled.

She looked back, her eyes momentarily locking on mine, but continued on and out through the door.

I tried making my way past the bodies bottlenecking at the exit, pulling students from the door. I needed to get outside, in front of the crowd.

"Adrian, don't," I said, grabbing his arm. He was shoving his way past two others and trying to squeeze between a female student and the door jamb. He shook off my arm, wiggled through the door, and disappeared into the rapidly growing mass of students.

I could see through the door's window that two deans had made it past the rush of the crowd and were moving briskly up the sidewalk toward the corner, communicating in rapid-fire over their two-ways, voices barking back and forth.

"They're about fifty yards from the corner."

"You behind them?"

"Right on them."

"Stay on them."

"Try to break up the crowd, separate if possible."

The frenzied crowd at the door slowed me down, and the angry head of the snaking mob was nearly a hundred yards away from me now. There was nothing I could do. I watched from my classroom window as students, teachers, deans began closing in on each other. I could see a single police car parked near the corner. And across the street, near the convenience store, a small group of African-American students stood, waiting, pacing, their eyes on the charging crowd.

Street traffic was the only barrier keeping the groups apart, the palpable tension moving back and forth over the cars from one angry side to the other. Jim and a handful of deans had moved in front of the students on the school side of the intersection, blocking their forward motion. My classroom window muffled the sound, but I could hear Jim's voice, his hands gesturing in strong, sharp movements, his head accentuating his demands, as the deans stood firm, like guards, one using a stiff forearm to hold back a student.

I squinted to see which students were in the crowd. Distance made it difficult. I knew Elena was in the middle of it somewhere, but what about Diego? Lucia? Suzana? I prayed Adrian was not one of them. I feared his popularity, his charisma, could be manipulated for the wrong reasons.

The deans began breaking up the crowd, being careful not to be overly physical, not to show too much force, as Jim's commands rose above the students.

"Everyone. Now. Out, go, leave!"

Some students, there only to soak up the excitement and witness a fight, were already moving away from the corner on their own, sensing the verbal battle was unlikely to escalate into physical violence. Elena was one of them. She, along with several others, walked back toward the main entrance. I was relieved to see she was no longer at the intersection. But as the crowd on the school side slowly dispersed, the African-American students on the opposite side stood their ground, taunting their enemies.

"Pussies!"

"What's the matter, Mexican pricks? Scared?"

The students weren't on school property and there was nothing Jim or the deans could do. But, the police officer in the parked squad took control, demanding the boys move along, forcing them to walk away from the corner, north on the main road and out of view.

Many of the students eventually made their way back into the eighth grade hall to retrieve discarded books and coats. I stood at my door, listening for what I believed would be the animated reactions and descriptions of what came dangerously close to being a bloody afternoon. But it was oddly calm, many students surprisingly subdued, with only a few talking about anything at all—a recent episode of a Spanish language TV show, and a new song on the radio. It was as if nothing significant had happened that afternoon, nothing worth talking about.

"See you tomorrow, Mr. Berner," one student said, waving as she passed me to leave.

As the hall emptied and I moved back inside my classroom, I heard one more voice near my door.

"Mr. Berner?" There was Adrian, jacket in hand. "Hey, those guys getting suspended for what happened today?"

I was relieved to see him, happy he wasn't with the deans, or in Jim's office preparing paperwork for the inevitable punishments.

"Something's going to happen. Can't do what they did and just let it go," I said.

Adrian paused a moment, appearing to contemplate my words, his hand rubbing his chin. "Yeah, guess so."

"Everything okay?"

"I know you grabbed my arm and all, but you know I wasn't in on this, right?"

"I was hoping you weren't," I said. "And you weren't, right?"

"I wasn't, Mr. Berner. Promise."

I watched Adrian walk to the end of the hallway, out the door, and onto the concrete sidewalk toward the north parking lot and out of sight. Through my classroom window, I could see the corner where just minutes before there had been a near riot. Now, there was nothing. No crowd. No policeman. No hateful words. And on the school side of the intersection, I could see a single student, a girl wearing a black coat and carrying a small red school backpack, waiting for the traffic to ease enough to allow her to cross and walk home in what was fast becoming the dim light of a winter afternoon.

Chapter 13

Cowherd's students had been trapped in white or blue T-shirts and jeans for months. Even the administrators realized the students needed a break from the rigid dress code. A number of students had been disciplined following the near race fight, but Cowherd's administrators believed things had calmed down enough to allow students a little room to express themselves. Dress Up Day was a single day each school year when students could wear more traditional school clothing, even serious dress clothes—girls in blouses and skirts, boys in cheap suits. Despite the poverty, most students had something to put on for weddings or funerals, hand-me-downs from brothers and sisters. For many, the clothes they wore on this day were the most special clothes in their closets, the nicest things they owned. And for others, the clothes weren't theirs at all. They were mine.

"Mr. Berner, aren't we also allowed to come dressed up as someone?" one student asked on the day before Dress Up Day, assuming it was a Halloween style event.

"The rule is, guys, you can come dressed up or come with some theme in mind—dressing like a movie star or something, as long as it is still dressed up," I said.

Before leaving school, teachers were asked to announce the rules and regulations for the day—no revealing tops, no super-short skirts. And although it was never said out loud, we were told to be aware of the occasional student who may have had nothing to wear, nothing considered *dress up*, putting the student in a position to be ridiculed or teased.

"Can we come as you?" one student asked.

"Me?" I said.

"Yeah, you. I can wear a tie," he said, referring to my typical daily attire.

That ignited several bursts of enthusiasm.

"Yeah."

"Let's be Mr. Berner!"

"Can the girls do it, too?"

This was not what I was expecting.

"Well," I said, momentarily thinking the idea through. "I guess you could do that."

How could this work? What would it mean? How would the students pull this off? Would the administration be okay with it?

"Tell you what," I said, thinking rapidly through the possibilities. "I'll bring in a bunch of old ties I have at home, and you guys can wear them. Anyone who wants to."

"That's cool."

"Do we all get them?"

Were the students setting me up? Was it a prank of some sort?

"I'll bring in as many as I can. I can't promise a tie for everyone, though. Work with me on this."

The following morning I carried in over a dozen ties—old ones, new ones, paisleys with garish patterns, wide and thin, a couple of them worn and frayed, and one with a brown mustard stain.

"I've got the ties," I told my first period students just before the start of class, tossing them on an empty desk in the front row.

"I don't have a tie for everyone who wants one, so here's

what we'll do. You don't get a tie if you're already dressed up, and those who are left will pick a number. Get the right number, you get a tie to wear."

Students stretched their arms into the air, waving their hands, standing up, trying to get closer to the mound of ties.

"I want one!"

"Please, I asked yesterday!"

"Over here, over here!"

"Easy, easy, guys," I said.

Students barked out numbers, trying to guess correctly, and I tossed the ties to the winners one by one. They wrapped them around their necks like scarves or their heads like headbands. No one had the slightest idea of how to tie a tie, so I stood before the class, working through the loops and twists. It didn't work so well, and I ended up tying nearly all of them myself, looping them like lassos over their heads. Eleven ties in all, with one saved for Rosa.

Rosa had been in one of my two language arts classes, but was forced to transfer to the other eighth grade team. The school deans believed she needed to get away from some of the other girl students on my team. Rosa had the personality of a bouquet of marigolds, pleasant but earthy. She could be sweet, but also bawdy, headstrong. Rosa said exactly what she thought with no filter, and tended to flirt a lot with the boys, something the girls didn't like much, creating friction and even a few hallway screaming matches. Rosa also had a turbulent home life. Her mother was believed to be in jail, her father was missing from her life, and many teachers were under the impression that Rosa was home alone a great deal during the late afternoons and evenings. She was seeing a school counselor a couple of days a week. And she didn't like that she had been transferred.

"I miss you, Mr. Berner," she would say.

"I miss you, too, Rosa."

When Rosa heard about the ties the day before Dress Up Day, she made it a point to stop by my classroom on her way out of school.

"You better keep one of those ties for me, Mr. Berner."

"Rosa, you really want to wear one? Aren't you going to wear a dress or something tomorrow?" I asked.

"I want the tie. I want to do the tie thing," she said, excitedly, insisting on being a part of the necktie group.

"Deal," I said. "But you have to wear it all day." That was the school rule. No changing.

Rosa looked older, more mature than she was and far from shy about her emerging sexuality. Several times she was caught necking in the halls with boys. I wondered if giving her a tie might keep her from wearing something too revealing on Dress Up Day, keeping her out of the assistant principal's office.

"Mr. Berner! Mr. Berner!" Rosa said, running toward me as I stood in my classroom doorway during the passing period between the second and third classes of the day.

"You got that tie, don't you?"

"Got it right here."

I handed her a preppy, green and blue striped tie, one you might see on a young boy at a New England boarding school. It was already knotted and ready to go.

"This is so cool," she said, slipping it over her head and giggling. Without missing a beat, she walked quickly, nearly skipping down the hallway.

"You know, I love you, Mr. Berner," Rosa said, playfully from over her shoulder.

I watched her stop at a row of lockers at the far end of the hall, fingering and flipping the tie as she showed it off to other students, then disappearing through the double doors into the school's main corridor.

Throughout the day students could be seen coming in and out of classes wearing the ties. Some knotted more tightly around their necks, others loose and dangling.

"What's with the ties?" teachers asked.

"Oh, they just wanted to be me, I guess," I said, having no other real explanation. Even Carol, the principal, came by my classroom during my preparation period after lunch to ask what was going on.

"Did they just ask you for them?" Carol said.

"Yep, their idea," I said. "I'm surprised they've kept them on this long."

I was concerned she might not like this much, tell me I shouldn't have brought the ties in to school, tell me I was breaking some rule or code, or that one of the students did something with one of the ties, something they shouldn't have—thrown it at a teacher, tried to strangle a kid.

"We should get a picture of them with you, wearing the ties. Don't you think?" Carol said.

"A picture?"

"Yeah, it would be fun," she said, moving a little closer and smiling. "You know why they're doing this, don't you?"

I was beginning to understand it now, but was embarrassed to admit it.

"They like you, Mr. Berner. No, they love you," Carol said. "You've made quite an impact."

The final period of the day was my eighth grade team's meeting time when we gathered together to discuss student problems and issues. We finished up early and I was alone in my classroom working at my desk when my cell phone rang.

"David?"

"Hey, what's up?" I said, recognizing my sister's voice. She was calling at an unexpected time.

"What are you doing?" she asked, sounding as if this was just a preparatory question, a buffer for what would come next.

"School's almost over. Finishing up some lesson plans. Everything all right?" I hesitated asking the question.

Slowly, distinctly she said what I most feared. "I think you should try to get here soon."

"What's going on?" I asked, already knowing the answer.

"It's not good, David. He's not good."

"What are the hospice people telling you? What do they think?"

"Day or two, they figure."

"He in any pain?"

119

"They say, no. He's out of it, Dave, I don't know if he even hears us anymore."

"I'll leave tonight, drive, stay in Toledo, and be there to-morrow morning."

"I would leave as soon as you can," she said more urgently.

"How's Mom?"

"She's pretty steady, David. Pretty strong."

"I'll call you when I get to Toledo to see how things are. Hang in there."

I hung up the phone and stared out the west side window of my classroom where the afternoon sun created long shadows across the school's front walkway. It was as if everyone in the world had disappeared. And in several parallel moments, my mind, every cell of my brain, was rapidly filling up with memories of my father—sitting in the stands at my Little League baseball games, showing me how to hook a worm on a fishing pole, taking car trips to Lake Erie's beaches, watching me play trombone in the high school band concerts, and recite my lines at the drama performances of *Our Town* and *Don't Drink the Water*. I saw his face, his ever-present bucket hat, and his hands. Dad's hands were thick and strong. Working man hands. I could see him using them to change the brakes on his old Chevy, to repair my ten-speed English racing bike, to dig a grave under the front yard's pine trees for the family dog, to build the cabinets and furniture that filled my parents' home, to play his favorite song—*Five-foot-two, eyes of blue...has anybody seen my gal*—on his old ukulele, and to tie his ties, the ones he wore every day of the twenty-five years he sold insurance for a living. Later in life, when he worked in home repair and carpentry, ties were not often part of his life. But before that, it was a suit or sport coat and a tie every workday. And when it came time for me to wear a necktie, Dad was the one who showed me how to knot it, turning my back to his chest, patiently moving my hands with his, making the motions that compose the perfect half-Windsor.

A call from the doorway halted the flow of memories.

"Mr. Berner," Rosa said as she stood at the classroom's entrance, yanking the tie up and over her head and pitching it to me. "Thanks. It was fun."

"Glad to hear it, Rosa."

"Love you, Mr. Berner," she said, turning and dissolving into the increasingly noisy hallway and the river of students heading for lockers, exits, and home.

I tossed the tie in my briefcase, gathered up my grade book and student papers, and put on my jacket. I was on my way home to pack clothes, load the car, and get on the road to begin the long drive east before dark.

Chapter 14

Dad was in the fetal position, his legs nearly pulled tight to his waist and his arms wrapped around his knees. His mouth was slightly open, his eyes glassy, staring into nothing. He appeared to be in pain, but his home hospice nurse insisted this was a stage where any pain wasn't registering. What was left of Dad's once stocky, muscular body was now just bones and flesh entangled in the white sheets of a cold, metal hospital-style bed, one that sickness forced into his home in the final months. It replaced the blond wood queen bed he and my mother bought just weeks after they were married over fifty years before.

"I love you, Dad," I whispered into his ear.

"I love you, Dave," he said, in a low, muted voice, struggling to find the breath to speak.

Those were the last words he said to me, and maybe the last words he said to anyone. For four days following that brief exchange, he remained, in essence, frozen, his eyes rarely blinking. The hospice nurse who came to the home several times a day said his organs were failing. Still, Dad hung on, living longer than previous patients at this stage of dying, defying the nurse's experience.

I considered returning to school as the vigil continued. There were times it seemed Dad would be in this state indefinitely. But the night before I was to head back to Chicago, while I sat with my mother in the soft evening light of her modest living room, in the darkened upstairs bedroom, Dad gave up.

"David!" I heard my sister call moments after taking the steps to his bedroom for what had become a routine evening check on him. "He's gone, Dad's gone."

I rushed up the steps and into the bedroom. Why I rushed, I don't know. Hurrying to him wasn't going to keep him alive.

Inside the room, my sister held his hand, looking into his lifeless eyes.

"Oh Dad, Dad," she moaned, stroking his cheek. "It's over, Dad. No more pain."

"Norman," my mother sighed as she reached for his hand.

I touched his head, kissed his forehead, and stood motionless. All the waiting and inevitability, all the months of care and worry, all the tears and fears had vanished. There was a palpable void, emptiness. Strangely, death from a disease like this can be empowering to those left behind. The disease wins, but the struggles are over for everyone.

I grew up on a hilly street in Baldwin Borough, a blue-collar suburb of Pittsburgh, where we played in the woods across the street, gathered friends for pick-up baseball in the field near the marked graves in the old Greek Orthodox cemetery just on the other side of the big cherry trees that bordered the woods, and tossed fallen green apples from my parents' backyard tree into the neighbor's chimney. Our house sat above the one next to it; slightly elevated because of the steep hill we lived on, making the chimney's hole an easy target from our home's side porch. We mostly missed, but a few made it. The neighbors, who many years later told us they knew we were tossing apples, never complained, never told our parents, never came out of their house to yell at the mischievous kids.

My father grew up in a house just eight houses away from my boyhood home, and Mom lived in a house just up the street, separated from Dad by just a few homes and a patch of Pennsylvania woods. In the 1940s and early 50s, Vernon Avenue was much more remote, almost rural. As a young boy, Dad even trapped fox nearby. It was considered "the country" even though the city's steel mills sat just a few miles over the tree-covered hills.

Growing up during the post Depression years also branded my father's personality. Throughout this life, Dad held onto things, couldn't throw anything away. Dad believed nearly everything could be used more than once; everything could get a new life. "If you throw it out," he would say, "then you'd have to say good-bye." Dad was never good with good-byes. He hated it when I left to go back to college after visiting over the holidays. When we traveled together to Scotland to play golf, my father's retirement gift, he fought back tears at the hotel in Glasgow when my flight schedule forced me to leave a day earlier than him.

Maybe all the good-byes were tough for Dad because of what happened when he was young.

When Dad was a teenager, his father left home for another woman, forcing Dad to quit high school and go to work. For decades, the two didn't speak. And when they finally did again, it was too late to fix the lost years. His father, from his deathbed in a Pittsburgh hospital, asked to see my dad. Dad never talked about what they said to each other behind the closed hospital room door, and no one ever asked.

A month following the funeral, I came back to Pittsburgh to help clear out Dad's things. Some of it Mom did not want touched—his shirts hanging in the hall closet, the top drawer of his dresser where he kept coins, a penknife, golf tees, and photographs.

"I still feel him, David, smell him. He's all around me," Mom said, pressing one of Dad's white golf shirts to her face.

But there was one spot in the house that Mom insisted had

to be attended to—Dad's basement workshop.

"It's so damp in there. It smells like an old garage. I would really like to get some of that junk out of the room," she said, grabbing my hand. "But I know it'll be hard."

My sister refused to do the job. "Too emotional. I can't do it," she said. So, I agreed to take on the task of cleaning out Dad's side of the basement, and most specifically, the workshop. But, I wasn't looking forward to how physically close I would have to get to what was in the shop, the rusted and broken things that Dad had oddly cherished.

On one shelf in the back end of the basement, next to Dad's overflowing green leather golf shag bag and above the old rusted golf clubs, sat a pair of blue golf shoes. Not dark blue or navy, but an awful aqua. And not *dyed* blue, but *painted* blue. It was Dad's handiwork from the mid-1960s when professional golfer Doug Sanders wore brightly colored pants and sweaters and matching shoes on the PGA Tour. Doug was Mr. Color in a black-and-white world. Somewhere, at the bottom of a dresser drawer, Dad must have owned an aqua blue golf shirt and aqua blue pants.

Throwing out some of the junk in my father's basement was relatively painless, physically and emotionally. And the dozens of golf clubs and hundreds of balls could be put to use by my sons or me. But some of what remained, well, I simply didn't have the heart to put out on the curb. It was like throwing away pieces of my father.

I kept the blue shoes.

Just opposite the basement shelves was the door to a sanctuary of sorts, and behind it was the workshop. I could still see Dad standing in the small space, reveling in the chaos before him.

"When you die, Dad, we're going to just brick up that room. I'm not going in there," I joked.

This room was not a place for the timid. It was once a coal cellar, only about five by three feet, and converted into a man's personal hardware store. Dad built a workbench and all around it haphazardly stuffed and stacked a lifetime of nails, screws,

David W. Berner

nuts and bolts, washers, overused tools, parts from appliances and clocks, old plumbing fixtures, and everything else my father would never, ever, consider throwing away.

"You never know when you'll need one of these," he would say as he proudly held up some odd piece of something.

What the hell is that? I would think, but rarely say out loud. Instead, I would smile, shake my head, knowing that having that little piece of hardware that fit perfectly into *something* was what made Dad proud. It was part of his own personal process of caring for the house and the family he loved.

He also was a pack rat.

Along the back of the workbench sat dozens of coffee cans loaded with finishing nails, masonry nails, screws, and bolts so badly rusted inside the Maxwell House containers that some had rusted into one unit. There were at least a dozen of the house's original electrical outlet plates, a heavy black rotary phone, the kind you see in a Humphrey Bogart movie, and on the wall a nuts and bolts holder fashioned from baby food jars—a project from my junior high school metal shop. And underneath the workbench was a canister-shaped cylinder of some kind with two wires jutting out of it and a flange around the bottom. I had no idea what it was. But whatever it was, Dad had two of them.

Scattered around the shop were four hammers, as many as ten screwdrivers, six pairs of pliers, and dozens of other assorted tools, mystery tools with purposes unknown. Wire of every gauge and length was neatly gathered into a roll and hung from nails hammered into the wall. Vise grips and clamps of all sizes leaned against the concrete sidewall. There were several cans and peanut butter jars of paint, many of them unlabeled, holding paint that had turned to colored stone. Paintbrushes littered the under-shelf below the bench, some delicately cared for and others worn, with bristles as hard as the handles.

Several times during the work, I found myself apologizing to Dad for throwing away anything from his shop he never would have.

"Sorry, Dad," I said out loud. "This has got to go."

As I slowly filled up two large garbage cans, I thought about how I had been trying to clean out my own personal, emotional workshop. How I was working to toss out what had become useless, rusted, and old, and wrestling to decide what to hold onto. I was clearing out the debris in my life—my old career and the debilitating malaise that had followed—and filling the void with new work, a new career, and maybe a new me. Dad never would have taken on this kind of personal project in his own life, but would have trusted and supported my need to reassess and redefine myself. Dad would have known how much his son needed renewal.

When the job was completed, I stood back from the shop and surveyed my work.

"Hope you like it, Dad," I said.

I pulled the cord to turn off the flickering fluorescent light and closed the door.

Chapter 15

I stood, once again, at my classroom door, watching my wing of the school fill with students. My father was buried, and I was back at Cowherd.

"Mr. Berner, too bad about your dad," said Adrian as he walked by, slowing down, but not actually stopping.

"Thank you, Adrian, I appreciate it."

"You still sad?" he asked.

"Yes, I'm still sad. Probably always will be."

Adrian smiled nervously and merged into the now flowing crowd of student bodies packing the corridor before the morning's first class.

"Mr. Berner, I'm so glad you're back. That substitute we had was an idiot," said Lucia. "No, he was an asshole. He talked about his days in Vietnam the entire time. Weird."

"Vietnam, huh?"

"Yeah, and he told us we needed to shut up a lot."

The pool of substitutes in the district was a scary group, and I was certain to hear more about this one.

On the large classroom blackboard students had left a chalk-written message.

WELCOME BACK. WE MISSED YOU.

Each had signed their name below it.

Before class began, Suzana handed me a sympathy greeting card with the photo of flowers and a candle on the front. All the students had signed it. I'm sure the teachers on my team had coordinated the effort, but the simple written sentiments were very much the students'.

I hope you're not sad.

Think good things.

We love you.

"Thank you, guys. It really is very nice," I told them after reading the messages to myself, feeling faint from the rush of grief that takes so long to understand and manage. The eyes of the students were on me. I steadied myself, cleared my throat, and tried to keep my emotional feet on the floor. "So, how was it without me?"

Nearly all of them began talking at once in a barrage of words and gestures, loud and animated, joining Lucia's earlier comments about the Vietnam substitute.

"You can't go away again, Mr. Berner," said one student. "We can't have that guy back."

"Tell the principal about him," another said. "He was just stupid."

Comments like this just kept coming, each one on top of the next. I put up my hands, palms facing them, trying to quiet them.

"I think I get your message. I promise, I'll ask the office about him."

The substitute, who had been hired at Cowherd in the past, apparently spent much of his time in the classroom telling students about the days he was lost in the jungles of Vietnam during the war, the times he killed Vietcong, even showing students his scars. There were several of the district's registered substitutes who refused to report when they were called to work at Cowherd, and others coming in for the first time were known to leave within hours. Just walk out. But the Vietnam substitute seemed to relish the edgy give and take with Cowherd's students. Plus, Cowherd may have been the only school that needed him enough to tolerate his strange behavior and his war stories.

The school couldn't necessarily be choosy about full-time faculty, either. But that didn't seem to matter when it came to one of my fellow cohort members—Nora, the basketball coach, the seventh grade science teacher. The administration didn't want to deal with her anymore.

Nora had always been the first to challenge faculty in our cohort. She was good-hearted, but quick to anger. She also carried her rebel style and disdain for authority on her sleeve. Sometimes it served her well, but at Cowherd her approach was a disaster.

"It's getting ugly around here," Nora told me before an evening class at the college. "I don't get along with the teachers on my team. They're lazy, they just don't get it, and I just hate the way they talk about the kids, calling them fuckers and assholes and pricks."

The word was that Nora was rubbing people the wrong way. Her in-your-face style didn't work with the status-quo teachers who didn't like young, inexperienced teachers asking questions, judging their decisions, being a thorn. In her role as the girls' basketball coach, though, it was quite different. The students loved Nora, and the other teachers were very aware of it. The reason was simple: she supported her girls, encouraged them, and when their grades were slipping and they were in danger of being sidelined until their grades were up again, Nora would go to individual teachers to discuss what each student needed to do. She cared. But caring wasn't enough.

Nora was either clueless about playing the political games or simply refused to take part. And yes, there were a lot of political games going on. It wasn't corporate America, but Cowherd teachers had turf to protect, issues to wrestle with, and some had skeletons in their closets. One, who was still teaching, had been suspended once for doing nearly nothing in class, apparently getting away with it for years because she was a friend of a former principal. And sex always seemed to be an issue. There were rumors of love affairs, teachers sleeping with other teachers—married ones—rumors of homosexuality, teachers flirting with female students.

Nora also was caught up in the politics of a school on the watch list. Cowherd desperately needed to improve its state test scores to keep from being put on what essentially was probation under the federal No Child Left Behind Act. Probation meant a loss of federal or state funds, something the district could not afford. And administrators didn't need more headaches; they needed to see student improvement in basic skills. If Cowherd wasn't able to meet the standards, under the law the state could take control of the school. That could mean state inspectors coming into individual classrooms, and many feared it could also mean teacher firings.

Nora was fired in the middle of the spring semester, a highly unusual event. Nora said the administration accused her of being unwilling to work within the system or with other teachers, defying the wishes of the school district. The administration apparently believed getting rid of Nora immediately was best for the students and the school. Nora was bitter.

After Nora's dismissal, I found myself wrestling, once again, with why I was doing what I was doing. I thought I was becoming a good teacher and believed I was growing into a better one, but teacher mentors were few and far between, and I saw how the mistakes and indiscretions of teachers affected the students. School was supposed to be a safe haven, a place where role models encouraged and even inspired students. But it rarely worked that way. Not at Cowherd. Did I want to stay in this environment? Should I go back to my reporter days? Could I? And if I stayed in teaching, would I be able to improve at this work without a lot of good people around me? I knew the quality of some of Cowherd's teachers was certainly questionable. And there were times that I was appalled by the ignorance.

Consider what happened one afternoon in the faculty lunchroom.

"What war did they drop the H-bomb?" one teacher asked

during a cell phone conversation several of us overheard. She was trying to get answers to questions on a test or quiz she had been preparing for a seventh grade class. "Oh yeah, and who dropped it? Was it the Germans, or something?"

I thought I was hearing one side of a joke, or a teacher imitating an exchange she had encountered with a student in a social studies class. Unfortunately, I was wrong. This teacher was honestly asking this question, shamelessly, out loud, in front of others.

Teachers like that kept their jobs, and Nora was fired?

I'll bet the Vietnam substitute knew who dropped the H-bomb.

Chapter 16

Three girls huddled near a locker on the far end of the eighth grade hall. They gathered close, one hovering over another, each concentrating intensely.

"You have to do it quick. If you go slow, it's gonna hurt like hell," the third girl said in a whisper as she stepped back, observing.

It was between classes, and the hallway was busy with overflowing voices. This little gathering would have been easy to miss, if I had been less observant.

"Ladies, what's so interesting?" I asked, trying to lift my head above them to get a look.

They made no effort to respond to me.

"Hold her ear over. Stretch it out so you can get the needle in," the third girl said, directing the scene.

One girl was preparing to shove a long needle through the earlobe of another. There was already a hint of bleeding, apparently from an earlier failed attempt. And the girl whose ear was the target grimaced as she anxiously held a tissue near her face, anticipating more blood. The girl with the needle appeared unfazed, as if she had done this many times before.

"Whoa, hold on here. Girls, stop what you're doing. Stop right now," I said, trying to assert some authority.

The girls ignored me.

"Stick it in now," said the girl whose ear was the focus of this handiwork. And with that, the needle pierced the lobe all the way through to the other side. More blood leaked from the ear.

"Shit!" the girl screamed.

"Girls, back up," I said, pushing my way into the middle of the three.

The needle remained in the earlobe like a sword through its victim.

"You have to put your earring in now so it works," said one of the girls.

The students kept talking about the next stages in this operation as if I had never appeared, didn't exist.

"It shouldn't hurt very long," said the girl who had plunged the needle into her friend's skin.

"Ladies, what on earth are you thinking?" I said. "You can't just pierce someone's ear out in the middle of the hallway."

The girl with the hole in her lobe removed the needle and began trying to put her stud earring in place.

"It doesn't hurt anymore," she said. "Is it still bleeding?"

I sent her to the health office.

Nearly every day there was something at Cowherd that turned my head around. And although the hallway piercing was certainly something I never expected to confront, in comparison to other happenings, it was minor league. One morning we were warned to be alert to the emotions of one eighth grade boy whose family member may have been shot in the driveway of their home the night before. A substitute teacher's purse was stolen from inside a classroom. A student was caught selling grass in a stall of the boys' bathroom. And he was pretty tricky about it. The buyer would stuff money inside the toilet paper roller cylinder, and the dealer would replace it with the dope wrapped up in a plastic bag. Other teachers told me this was a practice that had been used before, even after the doors had been taken off the stalls to prevent just this sort of exchange.

Incident after incident added to the Cowherd reputation, and now with some seven months of teaching behind me, I was beginning to expect, almost anticipate, the next one. It wasn't that I was becoming callous or indifferent; I was simply becoming part of Cowherd. It was my life; it was now part of my psychological makeup. The gang story, the shooting story, the drug story, and the racial tensions were just part of the fabric of the place and now part of me. I began to see how a lifetime of these stories could shape someone, anyone, everyone—the students and the teachers. The Cowherd stories I shared with my children were no longer just stories, tales to tell, but were now part of my life, little pieces of what I had become.

The end of the spring semester was near, and despite the harsh realities of Cowherd, it was a good time for the students. This was the season for the end-of-the-year events—the eighth grade dance, the class trip to the huge amusement park, and the eighth grade graduation ceremony. The annual goal was to get through all of these without students getting lost, hurt, arrested, or showing up drunk. Each of which, I was told, had happened more than once in the past.

The most controversial of the year-end events was the graduation ceremony. The dropout rate was high in District 131. Some administrators estimated one out of every four students who attended East Aurora High did not graduate. With that troubling reality, no one wanted to give students the impression that eighth grade was the end of the line. Using the word *graduation* and holding a ceremony with caps and gowns wasn't what the administration wanted to do. But longtime teachers at Cowherd thought it was important to give students some sense of accomplishment. One compromise was to hold what had come to be called the "Moving On" ceremony. Instead of focusing on the end of eighth grade, this ceremony would concentrate on students taking the next step toward high school and ultimately graduation. There would be no caps or gowns, only eighth grade certificates given out, not unlike diplomas. But the word *graduation* would simply not be used.

This was an exercise in semantics, but an important exercise. Many of the parents of our students had never finished school, and there were some who saw little reason for their children to finish. It was more important for their sons and daughters to get a job and help add income to the family. For many of the Mexican immigrants, some from families of migrant workers, formal education was not a top priority, and for a number of past students, eighth grade was the end of the educational line. When they turned sixteen, they would leave the classroom and begin filling out job application forms. The cycle wasn't going to be broken simply by changing the name of the ceremony.

Then there was the trip to Great America, the big amusement park. In past years, students snuck liquor on the bus and got drunk, there was an incident of shoplifting at the amusement park gift shop, and two students snuck back to the bus to conduct a little sexual exploration. Still, many teachers believed strongly that most of the students deserved the trip, and fought openly with the administration to make it happen. Money was an issue. Our financially strapped school district wasn't going to pay for it, and most students' families certainly couldn't afford it. Through a combination of teacher donations, small student candy-selling fund-raisers, and a student car wash, our eighth grade team was able to gather enough cash to keep down the cost for the students. Still, some couldn't afford the twenty-five dollars. Even with a number of anonymous donations from teachers and school staffers, we weren't able to help every student. There were at least twenty who had to stay back in the classrooms.

Of the three events, the eighth grade dance was the one most students anticipated. And again, money was an issue. Not the cost of attending, but the cost of looking the part. The girls wanted to wear prom-like dresses, but most could not afford them. Some would wear a sister's dress or a mother's hand-me-down, but for dozens of girls the daily school T-shirt and jeans were the best they could do.

But someone had an idea.

Teachers and staff donated dresses from their own closets.

Black, white, pink, gray, short, long, and frilly dresses arrived daily to the school in bags and on hangers. There were former bridesmaid dresses that had been worn once, dresses that no longer fit their original owners, and outdated numbers that had disappeared from the fashion pages. In a week's time, the school had over thirty dresses. The next step: to distribute them fairly.

We decided to hold an auction.

Students would be able to earn special tickets awarded for a good grade on a test, being helpful to other students, good attendance, whatever a teacher deemed would be appropriate. Students would then use those awarded tickets to bid on the dresses. By the afternoon of the auction we had some twenty-five girls with tickets in their hands, some holding as many as ten.

"This one, with its blue accents and classic neckline, looks superb with my eyes," said Mr. Cruz, holding up one of the dresses to his frame and doing his best fashion model imitation.

The auction was held after school in one of the eighth grade classrooms, and Mr. Cruz and I decided to have a little fun with the event.

"And this black number goes great with my bald head," I said, strutting and flaunting my stuff, giving the girls a laugh.

I camped it up as best I could, but Mr. Cruz was a far better model than me. He looked like he had done this before. I didn't ask.

In the end, every one of those girls walked out with something to wear to the dance. This was a time when I believed there was hope for Cowherd, its students, and its teachers.

Much of what happened at the school in those last few weeks became wired into my psyche. All that had seemed foreign months ago now felt oddly normal. Less than a year ago, I was clueless about what I was getting into, where my life was headed. But Cowherd and its students had made a mark on me, a cattle brand seared into my soul. My own children noticed it. Marie saw it. I was thinking less about myself, and more about those around me. It seemed trite, cliché, but the less I thought about me, the better person I became. One year ago, if you had told me modeling fancy dresses in an eighth grade student auction would put such a smile on my face, I would not have believed a word of it.

As I walked toward the parking lot the night after the auction, I saw two students on the far side of the school property.

"Hey, Mr. Berner!" they called from the end of the lot, vigorously waving their hands. I had met the two girls while substituting in a math class a few weeks ago.

"Hey, girls," I said. "Everything good?"

"Awesome, Mr. Berner," they said, nearly in unison.

"Heard about you and the dresses," one said, in an exaggerated feminine voice. "We heard you were *gorgeous*."

"Pretty hot, huh," I said, standing next to my car and putting my hand on my hip like a New York City runway model.

The girls giggled as they walked toward the street corner and away from the school. I waved a final time and pushed the electronic lock button on my keychain to open my car door, turned on the air-conditioning—it had been an unusually warm spring day—and plugged in my cell phone. On came the flashing light, the indicator that signals a waiting voice mail message. My heart jumped and sank at the same time.

Columbia College had called.

Chapter 17

Late at night, unable to sleep, I flipped through the TV channels and stumbled on a clip from a documentary about the 1960s. There was Bob Dylan accepting a humanitarian award sometime in the early part of the decade when he was still singing with the folkies, super thin, like a wiry teenager. He told the crowd that despite his tender years, somewhere around twenty-one, it took him "a long time to get young." Those words rumbled inside me. I think I knew what he meant. Sometimes it takes years, struggles, hard times, setbacks, and disappointments to get to a place where you believe you're supposed to be, where you feel you've found your place, where you have hope again.

I believed I was getting close to that place.

Sure, I wanted my marriage to survive, and I ached for my children and worried every day how all of what was going on with Marie and me was shaping them. My father's death was still painfully fresh, and I'd find myself fighting tears at odd moments in the day. But teaching had given me a new passion. And now, Columbia College wanted me.

The chair of the Radio Department interviewed me over the

phone for the full-time faculty position opening in the fall. This was a job my head wanted, but my heart wrestled with. Cowherd had put its arms around me, and I had put mine around it. The experience had given me new beginnings, enlivened my spirit, awakened what had become numb. I knew the money would be better at the college level, but Cowherd had given me far more than money could.

Despite uncertainties, I put everything I had into the twenty-minute phone interview. And when I was asked, "Do you want this job?" I paused only for a moment. "Yes," I said, even though "maybe" was probably the truer response. I was told the next step would be a search committee interview and a teaching session where I would be asked to conduct a class and be observed by tenured faculty and the department's chair.

Springtime at school, any school, can be tough going. Minds wander when the weather begins to turn. Concentration is in question, attention spans narrow, and that's true for teachers as well. When I saw interest waning, I wouldn't always fight it.

"Starting to get nice enough to go hit the white ball," I said to the students during a break in a reading assignment. I took the class outside to read on one particularly spectacular afternoon, when the sun was warm and a slight breeze from the north seemed to embrace the day.

The students knew my love for the game of golf and about the freelance writing I was publishing on the sport. I had shown them some of my work on the Internet as a motivation tool.

"What's with this golf?" asked Emilio, a boy who had little interest in much of anything all year. "How come you like this game?"

Most of the students had absolutely no connection to the game of golf. Historically, golf in Mexico had been very much a game for the elite, a rich man's sport. But, when you teach, you are keenly aware that exposing a student to something they have never experienced can sometimes fan new enthusiasm. Maybe Emilio would find golf was his game.

Emilio's family had strong ties to Durango, a mountainous part of Mexico where farming is the major occupation, and scorpions are plentiful. But it's also the setting for a song Bob Dylan co-wrote with Jacques Levy in 1976 called "Romance Durango," and it's where actor John Candy died, a heart attack while filming his last movie. During breaks in the school year, Emilio and his family would drive some two thousand miles from Chicago to this region of Mexico to see cousins, sisters, aunts, grandmothers. Family came first, as it did for many of my students, and sometimes Emilio would leave several days before the school break and return several days after classes had started again. In the days following spring break, students who had made their trips to Mexico came trickling back into class. One of them was Emilio.

"Mr. Berner, remember when you asked me if I was related to that golfer girl?" he said. Emilio's last name was the same as a star player on the women's professional golf tour, the LPGA.

"Well, my mother says we don't know no golfers. My whole family doesn't know no golfers."

"*Any* golfers."

"What?"

"Forget it. So, no golf in your family, huh?"

"I don't know nothing about golf. I see it on TV, though."

"It's a good sport," I said. "I like it. It takes strong mental concentration."

Emilio paused, hesitated, and then looked around as if he was making sure no one else was listening.

"You think you could teach me?"

I was surprised and delighted by the question.

"You want to learn to play golf?" I asked.

"Yeah, I see that guy Tiger and he's pretty good."

"Oh yeah, he's really good, Emilio. But it takes exceptional talent and years of hard work just to be a shadow of Tiger."

He hesitated again.

"I just thought it might be fun to hit the ball around."

"Tell you what," I said. "I have some old clubs in my garage. If you promise to give the game a shot, hit some balls in the park or in an empty field somewhere, I'll give you the clubs."

Emilio looked at me as if there was something I wasn't telling him, as if there were strings attached to this deal.

"Come on," he said with disbelief. "*Give* me them?"

"Sure, if you promise to use them."

"Well, shit. You bet. I'll take them. When can you bring them in?"

"I'll get them before the week is up. You'll have them for the weekend."

"Cool. That's cool."

I didn't really believe Emilio truly wanted the golf clubs. I assumed he was just curious. But two days later he was asking about them again. So, on Friday of that week, I handed Emilio eight rusty, scuffed-up clubs with worn and torn grips, wrapped together with three big rubber bands.

"Emilio, these are yours," I said.

He said nothing, looking only at the clubs—six irons, two woods—grabbing the bundle with both hands. He touched the clubs' heads, then ran his hands over the steel shafts and beat-up rubber grips.

"Have you ever swung a club, Emilio?"

Again, he said nothing, continuing to survey his set of sticks.

"It's sort of like baseball, in a way. But don't swing so hard," I said.

"I've never played baseball," he said, still looking the clubs over.

"Well, how about swinging a stick at a piñata?" I asked.

"You mean, whacking at something?"

"Yeah, in a way, whacking at something."

I pushed a few desks back, making some space in the classroom.

"Here," I said, sliding out a seven-iron from the grips of the bands. "Take the club back slowly, keep your head and feet relatively still, and swing through the ball. You won't have to swing super hard. But you do have to, well, *whack it*."

Emilio wound up and took a chaotic swing, just missing my leg and arm, and nearly embedding the head of the club in the wall. A second swing sent the club head smashing into a desk on the backswing and a chair on the follow-through.

I put my hand out to protect myself.

"Do me a favor, Emilio. Don't swing the club in your house. Swing it outside only. Got it?"

He tried to take another swing.

"Emilio. Outside."

"Cool," he said, taking another club from the bundle, examining it.

"Have fun," I said.

"Yeah, yeah. Cool." Emilio walked out of the room and into the hall, clubs in hand.

It was a couple of days later when I got the news that Emilio's golf career was already over.

"Have you hit some balls?" I asked.

"Yeah, I did, but my mother has the clubs now."

"Your mother?"

"Yeah, she wasn't too happy I was hitting balls."

"But, Emilio, I don't understand. She doesn't like you playing golf?" I asked, worrying I had breached some parental, cultural, or social rule.

"I broke a lamp," he said, hiding his mouth behind his fingers, laughing as if he had gotten away with something.

Somehow the broken lamp seemed worth it.

On Monday of the following week, I took a personal day and spent the afternoon at Columbia. I taught a class, was interviewed before a panel of tenured faculty, met with the school's dean, and ate a pleasant lunch of sandwiches and Coke in the Radio Department's conference room.

A week later, I was offered the job—a tenure-track position in the School of Media Arts.

Chapter 18

I always considered bringing my guitar to Cowherd and somehow working music into a lesson. We had a discussion in a grad school class about the benefits of using music in the classroom, how those students who were attentive to music many times did better in math, and how music could create the right mood for writing assignments.

But I never got around to it.

It had been months since I picked up the guitar. The tips of my fingers had grown softer, and the calluses, the scars of constant playing, had nearly disappeared. Graduate school and the long days at Cowherd had encroached on my guitar time.

Maybe the coming summer would be different.

I may not have been ready to play in class, but students definitely would have been ready to listen. With just a few weeks left to the school year, students had only celebration and ceremony on their minds—the eighth grade dance, field trips, graduation preparation, and possibly the most anticipated event of the school year—the arrival of the school yearbooks.

When the books arrived, the students wanted nothing to do with anything else.

"You gonna give us time to sign them, Mr. Berner?" Elena asked, anxiously waiting for the answer as she quickly leafed through the book, scanning the photos.

"Sure," I said.

With what seemed only a second of passing time, students were out of their seats, pens in hand, eagerly passing yearbooks back and forth.

My junior and high school yearbooks—hardbacks with the years embossed on the spine—sat on a shelf at my mother's home. Many times when I visited, I'd pull one down and thumb through it, seeking out my old girlfriend's pictures. I wondered what she had done with her life, where she was, how growing up had changed her, if she was still as cute, her hair still so dark.

"Mr. Berner, would you write in my book?" Suzana asked.

"I would be happy to, Suzana, but you have to write in mine," I said. I had also purchased a yearbook, somehow sensing its sentimental value well before Columbia College's offer.

"Hey, you better write in mine," said Elena from the back of the room.

A line of students formed in front of my desk, each waiting for me to sign their yearbook. Fifteen minutes quickly turned to thirty, and as I carefully considered the words I wrote, I thought about each student, wondering if I'd ever see any of them again.

"Thanks for writing, Mr. Berner," said Adrian. "You're a pretty good dude."

Some ten months earlier, when I first arrived at Cowherd, one student asked me a straightforward question.

"Why are you here?"

I didn't have a good answer for him then. And now, if the question was "Why are you *leaving*?" I'm not sure I would have had a good answer, either. There were teachers at Cowherd who stayed only as long as one school year, abandoning their jobs because they couldn't stand the place, the students, the poverty, and the struggles of the process. Some told students, very matter-of-factly, "I hate working here." It was outright rejection, but sadly, rejection students had become accustomed to.

Was I just like all of those other teachers? Was I abandoning these kids?

During the final period of the day, my preparation period, I was alone in my classroom. No students at their desks and no students in the halls of our wing. There was an eerie stillness, unusual for that time of the afternoon. It seemed unnatural. Out the window I could see the clouds moving across the horizon, a gray one and then a white one with slivers of blue cut between them. The changing sky was a sign of spring. And in front of me, on my desk, was my Cowherd yearbook filled with the words students had written.

You're one of the best teachers I ever had. Thanks for helping me.

You taught me so much. Thank you.

You're a really cool teacher. Stay that way.

And this from Suzana: *My favorite teacher that taught me a lot about what I think is going to be my career. All your advice and tips helped me with my writing. You made me love language arts.*

There were dozens like this, page after page, all of them humbling, and one in particular that came as a surprise.

Mr. Berner, a good teacher, that alwayz tried to help me, always—signed Elena Nicole Garcia.

A knock at my door interrupted my reading.

"We're going to meet now," said Mrs. Murray.

"Do you have a minute?" I asked. "And could you close the door?"

I hadn't planned to tell Margaret so soon about my plans, but I now felt compelled. It was as if I needed to reveal my departure to be sure the students' words written in my yearbook wouldn't change my mind.

"Margaret, I won't be here next year."

Her eyes widened. She stood still and erect.

"It was a hard decision, still is, but I got a job teaching college. Something I think I really want to do."

Margaret looked away only for a moment, and then turned her eyes back to mine as I continued explaining why I was leaving Cowherd.

"You have been great, and I love these kids. I really do. Something I never expected would happen to me. Margaret, this place changed me."

"You haven't told the kids yet, have you?" she said, wanting to be sure the students heard about this the best way possible. Margaret was always thinking of the kids.

"No, I'm not sure I should at all," I said. "Maybe you can tell students after graduation and if they come back to say hello. I just don't see the purpose in telling them now."

Margaret agreed.

"These kids like you a lot, Mr. Berner. They respect you. That's not easily done."

"Thank you, Margaret."

"It's nothing to be thanking anyone about, it just is. You connected. Most don't."

"I tried."

"You know, I didn't know if you were going to make it around here—showing up in that tie."

Margaret made me laugh.

"I never thought this opportunity for college would come so quickly," I said.

"You have a family. You have to think about them. You're not going to live on what they pay here. And frankly, I don't know how much longer I'll be around, either."

Margaret's husband, another teacher in another district, had been urging her to put away the books. She worked hard, harder than any of us.

"Oh, Margaret," I said, touching her shoulder. "You'll be here forever."

She shook her head slowly, reflecting on her own future.

"Let's meet in about ten minutes." She moved into the doorway and stopped. "You want to tell the rest of the team today?"

"Still got to tell Carol. I plan on doing that tomorrow morning, first thing."

Margaret disappeared into the hallway.

I put my hands in my pockets, leaned against the blackboard, and turned toward the only open window. Raindrops formed on the glass, clinging to the pane, some of them sprinkling in and falling to rest on the classroom floor.

Chapter 19

The next morning I arrived a half hour earlier than usual.

"Is Carol in yet?"

"Yeah, she's here. Don't know where, though. She's bopping around. You know her."

The longtime Cowherd receptionist held the phone against her ear as she ran through the early morning messages, absences, and late arrivals left on the school voice mail.

I hoped Carol was in her office working on something I could easily interrupt. I didn't want to prolong this, allowing emotions to get the better of me.

I grabbed my mail and sat in the lone lobby chair to wade through the mostly meaningless memos and letters, hoping to catch Carol as soon as she came back into the office.

"We had the book you did in your class out on the table there," the receptionist said, continuing to hold the phone to her ear, writing down messages.

"The Chicken Soup book?" I asked.

"Yeah, the one you did with the kids with their stories in it."

I had worked with students for over a month on publishing, albeit crudely, a student book of personal stories. The idea was for the kids to create their own *Chicken Soup for the Soul* book, a take-off on the popular series of inspirational books. We called it *Chicken Soup for the Eighth Grade Soul*.

"Carol wanted the parents who were waiting in the lobby to have a chance to see it and read it," she said.

There were nearly thirty short essays in the book, stories about friends and family, brothers and sisters stationed in Iraq, relatives far away in Mexico, gangs, crime, violence, the excitement of learning to drive, and the real and innocent heartbreak of first loves. One student created the artwork for the cover, a pencil drawing of a little boy carrying a book. The local Kinko's printed copies for all the students who contributed, giving each their very own "published" work.

"This is going to be a real book, Mr. Berner?" one student asked as they worked on their second and third drafts.

"Certainly not going to be as slick as a book in the library, but, yes, it will be a book, *your* book, all yours," I said.

"With our names on it, right?"

"With all of your names on it. You bet."

On the day they were handed out, students accepted them like prizes. In the hallways, they waved them like awards and stood at their lockers reading each other's stories.

I wasn't looking for recognition. After all, the real work came from the students. Still, to have the book displayed in the school's lobby was proof someone had liked what we had done. But, when I looked at the end table in the lobby that morning, hoping to see the book, it wasn't there.

The receptionist took the phone from her ear and put it back in the cradle.

"Too bad someone stole it," she said.

The school district administration wasn't going to be happy about my departure, and I anticipated a scolding for not finishing the job, not seeing things through. My graduate scholarship money was linked to my agreement to stay in the district, teaching for at least three years. I was about to break that promise, and certainly would be forced to pay back some of the money.

But, I had been over this in my mind many times before.

"Hey, Mr. Berner," a chorus of voices called from the doorway.

"Hey, girls. Hey, Adrian."

A group of students had come in a little early to help out with a sports-related pep rally scheduled for later that morning. One of them was Adrian, who appeared more animated than usual. Probably an attempt to show off to the seventh grade girls he was with. He even waved to me, something he rarely did. Adrian looked happy that morning. The girls did, too.

"Carol's in," said the receptionist. "I just saw her walk in her office."

I was nervous. Not because I didn't want to go through with it, but because I believed I was moments away from disappointing Carol. She had believed in me, asked me to be on the school improvement committee, liked what I had done, knew I would grow as a teacher, and now I was about to let her down. Not because I was some tremendous talent, some educational god, but because the school had hired me to do a job, and I was abandoning that duty.

"Carol, you got a minute?" I asked, sticking my head through the office doorway.

"Sure, Mr. Berner, come on in," she said through her perpetual smile.

"I have some news, and Carol, I have to tell you, it wasn't an easy decision. It wasn't easy at all."

I sat down in one of the two chairs facing the front of her oversized desk. She pushed away a bit from her side, letting the rollers on her chair separate her from the blotter, the books, and the ceramic pencil cup.

"Carol, I won't be back in the fall."

Carol's eyes squinted, mouthing "oh" as if experiencing unexpected pain.

"I got a position teaching college, and it's where I ultimately want to be. I just didn't believe I would find it this quickly."

I was surprised how the words came so easily.

"Mr. Berner," Carol sighed, "you're leaving us."

I said nothing, nodding my head.

"You're going to teach college," Carol said, confirming the news. Her words were coming more slowly, deliberately, her chair now closer to the desk, her elbows on the blotter with her hands folded together. "And this is a full-time, tenure-track faculty position?"

"Yes, it is, Carol." My face felt hot, the back of my neck wet, clammy.

"Wow," Carol said, pausing as if allowing my words to sink in. "And what college is this?"

"Columbia. In the city."

She paused again, and then Carol did what I never anticipated. Carol began to cry.

"Carol. Please," I said, reaching my hand across the desk to try and touch her arm.

"Oh, Mr. Berner. I'm happy for you."

"Carol, please. Please don't cry."

She pulled a tissue from the box on a nearby bookshelf, stood up, patted her face just below her eyes, and moved around her desk to my side.

"We are going to miss you, Mr. Berner. The kids are going to miss you," she said, reaching out to hug me. I stood to hug her back.

Carol wasn't crying because she was losing me, a novice teacher just finding his way. I was certain she was crying because the kids would again watch a teacher walk away from them, crying because she knew what a difficult job it was to keep teachers at Cowherd, ones who cared.

"I'm not going to disappear, Carol. I want to come back from time to time, say hello, maybe be part of career day, if you'll let me," I said. "I can't just walk away. I don't want to walk away."

"Mr. Berner, you are welcome here anytime," she said, one hand holding mine and the other still wiping tears.

For a few more minutes we talked about what it was like to

have a contract to teach at a college, about tenure, and what demanding experiences I would face. But Cowherd's first period was about to begin, and we both knew our talk had to come to a quick end. We walked together toward the door, stopping to look at the student artwork Carol displayed on her office wall.

"There's some real talent in those, isn't there?" I said, my eyes remaining on the strokes of colored paint.

"Yes, there is, Mr. Berner," said Carol. "All the talent in the world."

Chapter 20

There wasn't much chance of anyone accomplishing any schoolwork—not with so few classes remaining, the sun getting warmer, and our days numbered.

"You gonna party when school's over, mister?" asked Diego.

"Sure, Diego, I'm going to celebrate all of you going to the high school."

"Well, if you really want to party, I can get you a white bitch. You know, I *am* the pimp. You just let me know."

He slipped through the crowded morning hallway, his words trailing behind him, swallowed in the noise.

I was going to miss Diego.

We were just a few days away from Cowherd's graduation ceremony, and several students in our team were failing classes, all of them in jeopardy of returning to Cowherd for another year. However, there were not as many as I would have expected earlier in the school year. That's not to say they deserved to graduate. For a number of these students, graduation was a gift. These were good kids who had struggled for years, who would gain little by repeating a grade, and would likely be hurt socially, even culturally, if we held them back. Was it right? Should we have been more demanding, rigorous? One lesson I learned at Cowherd was how and why one should bend the rules, even break them now and then.

Two days before graduation, I walked into Cowherd at 6:30 on an overcast, chilly morning, finding the walls wider, the ceiling higher. The cavernous halls allowed the rustle of my nylon windbreaker to echo off the concrete block walls. I could hear the electronic churning of the single, unreliable copy machine in the office, where a student teacher was busy duplicating a class assignment. And at the far end of the hallway outside the gymnasium, nearly out of view, Enrique stood on a ladder, the scrape of his screwdriver prying at the metal fixture of a ceiling light in need of repair as I made my way past the doors of the first-floor classrooms.

I made my usual walk to the teacher mailboxes and then down the main hall to the eighth grade wing. Stepping through the double doors, I saw Mrs. Murray and Mr. Cruz standing alone outside a classroom talking softly. The creak of the doors and the rhythmic clicks of my footsteps on the tiled floor were amplified in the empty hallway of the slowly awakening school, enough for anyone to notice. But neither turned to acknowledge me. Mr. Cruz's head was down, eyes to the floor, as Mrs. Murray spoke softly, almost cautiously. It was unusual for either to be so hushed, even at this hour. She held a grade book in one hand and the local newspaper in the other.

"Mr. Berner, have you seen the *Beacon*?" The *Aurora Beacon* was Aurora's daily newspaper. She held it up, showing me the front page. "Adrian's mother. She's dead. Shot by her boyfriend."

I stopped in mid-stride. It was as if someone had turned off my nervous system, my muscles, leaving me immobile.

"Adrian was apparently in the house, in the room at the time," said Mrs. Murray, continuing like the staccato message of a telegram.

"Grandmother shot, too. She's in the hospital. Apparently

155

going to make it."

As softly as she spoke, Mrs. Murray's words still echoed off the walls, producing heat on my skin.

Margaret read the headline of the newspaper story out loud. "Fatal Shooting: Man Still in Custody." She folded the paper and handed it to me.

"You should read it before the kids come in," she said, her shoulders slumping, her face weary and pale. Margaret said she had spent much of the night making phone calls to police and school administrators, trying to find out more information about the shooting.

"We need to talk about how we're going to deal with them this morning," she said, nodding her head toward the glass doors and the students waiting on the other side.

Many students came early, sometimes an hour before the school's opening bell, dropped off by parents who were expected at their jobs.

I stared at the newspaper, the headline, the date on the upper left corner, as if that might validate the news I was hearing.

"How's Adrian?" I asked, my eyes still on the newspaper.

"He's okay, but apparently the boyfriend pistol-whipped him," said Margaret.

Leaning against the hallway wall, I read the newspaper's account.

Police on Tuesday continued to question a 31-year-old man suspected of killing his live-in girlfriend and wounding her mother during a domestic disturbance inside the couple's East Side apartment Monday night.

Although it was never reported anywhere, word was that Adrian was part of the struggle for the gun. There apparently had been a violent argument between his mother and her boyfriend, a weapon was pulled, and Adrian, acting out of fear, anger, and love for his mother, tried to wrestle it away from her boyfriend.

The man, whose name was not released, surrendered to police around 11:45 p.m. Monday after barricading himself inside a nearby home for nearly three hours after the shooting.

The boyfriend used the barrel of the gun to strike Adrian across the head, and then he shot Adrian's mother and his grandmother. It was believed Adrian saw it all. Why Adrian wasn't shot was a mystery. Maybe it was something about how he tried to defend his mother, the fearlessness in the face of a gun. Maybe the boyfriend didn't know how tough Adrian could be.

In February 2003, the man was charged with two counts of domestic battery after police said he struck her in the head and bit her on the arm. The charges were later dropped.

Unfortunately, this kind of violence was not unusual in East Aurora. Shootings, drug dealings, robberies, domestic trouble were all part of the regular police blotter. I knew this when I took the job at Cowherd, but I didn't think it would get so close, so raw.

"They argued a lot," said a neighbor who lives across the street from the couple's home in the 1600 block of Northeast Drive.

The woman was the mother to three middle-school-aged children and worked long hours at the Hollywood Casino to support them, the neighbor said.

Neighbors said Adrian's family had moved to Aurora three years ago to escape the gangs and troubles of Chicago. For her, the town of Aurora was at least better than the neighborhoods she knew in the city.

"The kids came No. 1 before anything for her," the neighbor said. "She was a good woman and a good mother. People around here can't believe she's gone."

I let the newspaper fall to my side and looked through the glass doors of the eighth grade wing. Students continued to gather there, but there was none of the usual laughter, chatter, jumping, shoving, book snatching. Instead, there were tears, quiet talking, with some students hearing the news for the first time. I avoided eye contact, trying to keep the sting below the surface.

When the school doors opened for the morning, the crowd was not eager to enter, like visitors to a wake. Students hugged each other at their lockers; others stood alone—one held her hand over her eyes.

"Mr. Berner, did you hear about Adrian?" Suzana asked in a whisper bordering on reverence.

"Yes, I have," I said, putting my hand on her shoulder.

"That is so sad," she said.

I stood by the classroom door as students found their seats. An uncomfortable stillness filled the room. It was several minutes before anyone spoke.

"What's Adrian going to do, Mr. Berner?" Lucia asked as several looked up from their desks, anxious to hear the response.

"Guys," I said, sitting down at an empty desk in the middle of the room, the students surrounding me. "I don't know."

They wanted me to tell them something good, something positive, give reassurance. They wanted me to tell them Adrian would be okay.

Lucia's question gave way to others.

"Where will he live?"

"Is he going to graduate?"

"Is he going to come back to school?"

"Will he be here today?"

"Did the police put the guy in jail?"

I wanted to have definitive answers, but I simply didn't. No one did.

"Police say someone's in custody," I said. "But I don't know any more than what the newspaper reported. Maybe Mrs. Goodman can answer some of the questions."

Carol was already at the door. Without a knock, a good morning, or a hello, she came straight in, stood at the front of the class, her hands clasped in front of her near her waist as if in prayer. She spoke to the students, her eyes red, her face flushed and blotchy.

"I know all of you are aware of the tragedy within our Cowherd family." She paused as her voice weakened. "This is not an easy morning and there are few details, very few answers I can give you. In fact, I don't have many answers for any of this."

Two students began to cry. Others remained still, motionless. Some looked away; one dropped her head into her hands.

"We can only offer Adrian as much support as we can. And we will do that. I know you will, too," Carol said, pulling a tissue out from her skirt pocket. "If any of you need time to speak with a counselor, to be alone, or even to call a parent for your own support, let us know. Let Mr. Berner know."

With that she turned to me, nodded, put her hand over her mouth, and wiped away tears with the other. She walked through the door, gently closing it behind her as if not wanting to disturb the inner thoughts, the emotions we were trying to control.

When I was just a boy, a distant cousin was shot and killed in Vietnam. I can still see his body in the dark oak casket and family crying near the flowers surrounding him. He wore his Marine dress blue uniform, shiny medals on his chest, and an American flag was crisply folded near his feet. His mother sat in the funeral home's upholstered, Victorian-style chair, so still she might have been dead herself while mourners came by to hold her hand, touch her shoulder, hand her tissues. Vietnam was far away for a nine-year-old boy, and my cousin was someone I seldom saw and barely knew. But it was my first visit with death, the first time I knelt before a body and prayed to God, the first time I saw people weep so hard they needed help to sit, to stand, to walk, the first time I remember seeing my mother cry.

I wondered if Adrian had ever seen his mother cry.

Chapter 21

On the day of graduation the students had a half day of school. We did little but play games in the classroom—checkers, chess, cards. We signed yearbooks and talked about the upcoming summer.

"I heard Adrian's going to be there tonight," Elena said.

"I hope so," I answered. "I'm sure his mother would have wanted him to be."

Students certainly wanted Adrian to take part in graduation, but many wondered how he could. His mother was dead. The funeral arrangements were being made. And students didn't know what to say to him or how to say it. What do you say to a friend whose mother has been shot dead?

The Moving-On Ceremony was held at the high school auditorium. It was a fairly elaborate presentation with several speakers, musicians, balloons, and awards, as well as a history, I was told, of rowdy crowds. The parents and families saw the ceremony as an opportunity to whoop it up, and many would cheer and yell out during the middle of the proceedings. The atmosphere was that of a sporting event, a Latin American soccer match. This was not graduation day at the local prep school. This was graduation day for Cowherd, for students whose parents never graduated from anything, some who never finished fifth grade. It seemed to me the families had a license to get a little rowdy. Their children didn't make it to this ceremony in the traditional way—why should we expect them to celebrate in the traditional way?

Graduation was either the beginning of the future or the beginning of the end for these students. They could grow from the experiences and blossom in high school, but the reality was that half of the students entering East High would never get a diploma. Many would work at McDonald's, as landscaping laborers, and at dead-end retail jobs. Some would become day laborers and migrant workers like their parents before them. Some would die from the violence of gangs. Some would die from drugs or alcohol. Others would walk straight from the school to the unemployment line and would fall into the circle of poverty.

But there would be success stories. Some students would choose the military. The conflicts in Iraq and Afghanistan were in their infancies but escalating, and despite statistics proving that America's poor make up much of the country's fighting forces and ultimately many of the casualties, students remained drawn to a serviceman's sense of belonging and camaraderie. There would also be a handful of students who would go to college and defy the odds of generations. But they would have to be nurtured and directed, assisted by teachers and counselors and family members who understood and cared.

Caring was uncommon. Cowherd's students had dreams like so many others of their age—to be pilots, nurses, TV reporters, veterinarians, beauticians, lawyers—but they rarely expressed those dreams. Goals were rarely discussed. Who in their lives had ever had goals, or dared to speak of them? Students like Suzana were never told they could be something other than a worker at the local fast-food restaurant. Suzana was a good writer. She wrote from her heart, telling stories of her brothers stationed in Iraq, about her fears and worries for them. But she didn't know she could write with such passion, never was told; no one ever noticed or cared to notice. I did. I told her. I helped get her placed in an advanced English Composition course at the high school. But she would need more than me. She would need other teachers, family, and friends. Suzana was a symbol of the hope that existed.

The auditorium was full. Families brought as many as ten members with them, despite being advised that four would be the limit. We let them in anyway. There were nearly a thousand people seated, with a hundred more leaning against the side walls. The students came dressed in the best they had. For some that meant the cleanest T-shirt. Before the ceremony, the auditorium reverberated with boisterous talk and shouts between families and former students who spotted each other in the crowd. Cameras flashed. Poses were struck. It was a party.

"Mr. Berner," said Mrs. Murray, whispering in my ear as I stood in the aisle watching the families take their seats. "We hear Adrian will be here, and may already be."

"He's coming?" I said, surprised to learn the rumor was true. "Do the students know?"

"They'll know soon."

School administrators had heard from Adrian's family that morning, and the word was being passed around to all the teachers on the eighth grade team. No one had seen him, yet.

The students were meeting in a large room to the left of the stage and placed in alphabetical order to be sure graduation certificates would be handed to the right student at the right time. I peeked inside the room to see if I could spot him.

"You seen Adrian?" I asked a student near the door.

"He supposed to be here?"

"That's the word."

"Unless he's way in the back, I haven't seen him."

No one would blame Adrian if he didn't make it.

Each of the teachers had a section of the auditorium to watch over, patrol, once the students entered. It was a way of keeping them focused and attentive to the ceremony. I was down front and stage left, not far from the door where the students would come in, single file, to their seats. When the double doors opened and students began to march in, the auditorium erupted with applause and deafening hoots and hollers. Students waved to the crowd, some did a little dance, and others moved with little emotion, seemingly stunned by the response.

I watched the faces as they entered the auditorium—Suzana, shyly smiling, her big round eyes full of pride; Sergio, flushed with the embarrassment that comes when stage lights shine and hundreds of eyes seem to be zeroing in on only you; and Diego, with his toothy grin, camping it up for maximum attention. There was Lucia wearing lipstick for the first time, and Rosa, as usual, overdoing the purple eye shadow, and Elena showing off a new necklace of fake gold and rhinestones. Hector had allowed the peach-fuzz stubble of a week's worth of adolescent beard to mature his chin, and Carlos's cheeks appeared bigger, almost cherubic, now that his parents had insisted on a graduation haircut, a buzz cut. The faces looked so innocent and yet so experienced, some so young, others far older than their years. I thought about my boys and the graduations to come. I prayed they'd find their way in the world, find what they were good at, passionate about, and wondered if their faces on graduation day would be windows to their souls. I wondered about my own face and how it must have looked to the students now, a face that had been with them for almost eight hours nearly every day, and would be soon gone.

The students kept coming and I kept watching.

Then Adrian stepped into view.

He was dressed in jeans and a white T-shirt, his arms motionless at his sides, his eyes slightly bloodshot and hollow, his expressionless face still stunned from a confrontation with the barrel of a handgun. Adrian glanced into the crowd, but unlike most of the students, he waved to no one, and lagged behind the other students as one does when there is no place in particular to go. I watched as he moved toward his seat, hoping I could get a sense, a signal of how he was holding up and if he was going to be all right today. But there was nothing. Whatever he was feeling was masked.

There were speeches from administrators, the kind you would expect, filled with phrases like "as you move forward to new challenges" and "this is your day to shine." I remember the school band playing what was probably a Sousa march in a simple major key, the trumpets hitting an occasional off-key note. Pomp and Circumstance was not part of the program, but the clarinets did squeak their way through something similarly ceremonial. Then, it was time for the graduation certificates and the calling of names. Each student was recognized with an announcement, a handshake, and the award of the eighth grade diploma. One by one the names were called and cheers from family and friends filled the air as each student came forward.

Adrian stepped center stage.

As he reached to take his certificate from the hand of our principal, the auditorium erupted. Students cheered, stamped their feet, and chanted his name.

"Adrian, Adrian, Adrian!"

One by one students rose to their feet, clapping until the entire eighth grade class was up, some standing on the chairs. The families in the audience followed, each row exploding with whistles and roars. The line for certificates stopped moving, and students stepped out of the procession to turn to Adrian and applaud. Carol pulled Adrian close to her side, appearing to whisper into his ear. He softly smiled and took a quick look out at a thousand people now giving him a standing ovation. Moving mechanically to his seat, Adrian returned his eyes to the crowd, appearing bewildered by the attention. He looked down at the certificate, then back to the crowd, as the noise continued to thunder through the auditorium.

"Adrian, Adrian, Adrian!"

I clapped along with them all, holding back tears others were shedding. I felt somehow I had to remain in control, stay strong, stoic. I thought of Adrian's mother, how she couldn't share this moment, how she couldn't put her arms around her boy and congratulate him, kiss him. Adrian would not celebrate as expected, far different than the plans his mother might have made. There would be no party, no homemade cake celebrating his accomplishments. Instead, his day would include time at the hospital to visit his wounded grandmother and a trip to the funeral home to pray for his mother.

The applause continued for many moments before the student line began to move again, the last certificates were handed out, and the band played its final songs.

"Good luck to all of you and congratulations," Carol announced to the students, sending them on their way to a new school, and prompting one more burst of applause from the crowd.

As students and families exited through the side door of the auditorium, I stood alone in the lobby, trying to avoid the inevitable hugs, lengthy good-byes, and well wishes. I wasn't brave enough for it. My body was depleted of sensation, of energy, as if I had been running, each drop of sweat marking the loss of emotional stability. I simply had to stay in control, and the one way I knew how to do that was to remain alone. Not only because I wanted to keep my distance, but because I needed to keep it for self-preservation. Still, I knew I could never truly detach myself from what Cowherd had given me.

Years ago, some time shortly after I completed my undergraduate degree, I read a book about Native American spirituality. I remember one particular passage about the belief that every time you say good-bye to someone, you take a piece of that person with you. I left the East Aurora High School auditorium that day with a lot of luggage.

After slipping out through the doors of the school without a word to anyone, I walked to the far end of the high school parking lot, beyond the concrete and into the grass field where the overflow of vehicles had been directed. It was a sunny day, but the early spring had left pockets of mud, and I stepped awkwardly around them, shimmying to keep my balance. I ached to look back at the school, at the students and families soon to be on their way to personal celebrations. But I couldn't.

My final good-bye could never be a simple handshake and a good luck wish; it could never be tied up in a perfect little bow.

I keyed the ignition of my car and heard the searing guitar and vocal intensity of The Rolling Stones' "Gimme Shelter" blare out of the radio. I cranked the volume, rolled down the windows, and pulled away, pretending to ignore the flashing images in the rearview mirror—my former students, certificates in hand, moving on with the rest of their lives.

Epilogue

The seventh-floor office at Columbia College looks out over Chicago's busy Congress Parkway in the city's South Loop. Across the street is one of the college's residence halls. Occasionally, I catch a student waving to me, and this morning one of them calls me on the phone.

"I can see you, Mr. Berner," the student says with a sneaky laugh.

It's all in fun.

It can be noisy at this end of campus. The deafening echoes of city traffic, the piercing police and ambulance sirens bounce off the tall buildings, and the heavy rattle of city trucks gain momentum in the canyons of Chicago's skyscrapers, resonate against the large window that looks out onto Congress Parkway. But there's peace in the turbulence and I've become accustomed to it, find it soothing. My office at Columbia is a comfortable place.

It is nearly seven months since I left Cowherd. The summer months between leaving East Aurora and coming to Columbia I fill with writing, some freelance broadcast work, golf, and time off with my boys. We go camping along the upper Mississippi, high on the bluffs in Wisconsin, visit *The Field of Dreams* across the river in Iowa where the Kevin Costner movie was filmed, and take a road trip back to Pennsylvania to see my mother. Casey helps me choose a new laptop computer, and Graham gives me a helping hand painting my new Columbia office. We agree on a modestly fashionable green, a sage color that is infinitely better than the dull, institutional beige applied nearly a dozen years before. We hang some artwork, including a print of dozens of antique radios sitting on a shelf, put up a promotional poster for the Third Coast Audio Festival held in Chicago each year, and another for the City Lights Bookstore in San Francisco. A photo of my children is placed on the back left corner of my desk, and a framed diploma from graduate school is hung on the wall near the window. When the work is complete, Graham and I celebrate the room's fresh look by buying cans of Diet Coke and submarine sandwiches, and sitting on the floor to eat them, christening the carpet with spilled yellow mustard.

On an early Monday morning in November, I prepare a lesson for my Ethics in Broadcasting class. In the current climate of broadcast industry deregulation, the class name seems an oxymoron, with concerns of questionable business practices and new payola scandals in radio. But, looking at it more positively, these issues are what educators call "teaching moments."

Taking a break to check e-mail, I comb my way through a myriad of college-generated announcements, departmental updates, Viagra spam, acid reflux remedies, and a reminder from my son Casey to pick up a white poster board at the grocery store on the way home, something he needs for a school project. I read a few selected e-mails and begin systematically deleting most of the rest until I come to one in particular. It's recent, the e-mail time stamp tells me it was sent just a few hours before, and what's in the subject and sender windows appears out of place with the others, yet there's a curious familiarity. In the subject box it simply reads "HI" and in the sender heading is the name "Suzana."

I know only one Suzana who spells it with a *z*.

hey mr. berner how have been doing??? its me Suzana. I hope you remember me. I went to cowherd on Tuesday for open house to look for you and you weren't there! Mrs. Morton told me that you got a new job at Columbia College. So I went to the website and I found you. Do you like it better over there? Hopefully you do. I like East a lot just because the days go by way faster. Its nothing like middle school. I wanted to thank you for putting me in the English honors class. I find it really easy and that's my favorite class (of course) but I have to go because im writing from school and its almost time to go. Bye take care please write back when you get the chance.
Suzana

Suzana!!!
Wow! I am so happy to hear from you. Your note made my day. I am so sorry I missed you at Cowherd when you visited. I would have loved to see you. I hope to stop by and visit later this school year and might be involved with the career day. I miss Cowherd, but I love my new work too.

It sounds like your high school experience is wonderful and I'm thrilled you like the honors English. You deserve to be there.

How are your brothers doing? Your family?

Please keep in touch. I will hold onto your e-mail and will definitely keep in touch with you. You were one of my favorite students…and you will remain one.

Tell your instructors I would love to speak

in their classes some day!

Let me know what you're up to and good luck this year.

Mr. Berner

Since that first e-mail, I've received several more from Suzana. She keeps me posted on her writing at school and her grades, her brothers' safe returns from Iraq, her work on the school newspaper. In one e-mail, Suzana asks for advice about what to do after high school. She hopes to be the first in her family to go to college.

The more I communicate with Suzana the more frequently I wonder about the futures of so many of my former students—Lucia, Elena, Diego, Adrian. For nine months I had been a daily part of their lives—they likely saw more of me than their own parents—and then it was all over. And although I knew it was unlikely I would see any of these students after graduation, Suzana and the others remain with me nearly every day, memories creeping into my mind unexpectedly in silent moments. Their presence, in many ways, is permanent, a tattoo.

Some might see Suzana's e-mails as a sign that I did my job as a teacher well enough that a student wanted to reconnect with me. Instead, I see them as a gift, freely and spontaneously given, a gift of simple words from a not so simple time when change opened my eyes and soul and taught me how life's plans are only that, just plans. Change is the only constant, and our days are far more accidental than any of us would have expected. You make your way through a long series of emotions, events, and encounters, each changing you a little, chipping away at the old you and building a new one, sometimes delicately, sometimes with brute force and recklessness. It's a continual reinvention of the core of your life, a necessary journey.

In my office, tacked to the wallboard above my desk, remains the printout of Suzana's first e-mail. I look at it every day.

CPSIA information can be obtained at www.ICGtesting.com
Printed in the USA
LVOW040440150812

R7015300001B/R70153PG293434LVX6B/3/P